THE JOURNEY TO BRING BACK PLAY

Copyright © 2022 by Nataša Ćećez-Sekulić

All rights reserved. No portion of this book may be used or reproduced, stored in any retrieval system, or transmitted in any form or by any means—electronic, mechanical, photocopy, recording, or otherwise—without prior written permission of the publisher. For information, contact Liminal World at info@natasacecezsekulic.com

ISBN: 978-1-7751681-2-6 (paperback)
ISBN: 978-1-7751681-3-3 (ebook)

Publisher: Liminal World, Victoria, British Columbia, Canada
Cover and Book design: Iryna Spica, www.spicabookdesign.com
Editor: Darcy Nybo, www.alwayswrite.ca

Printed and bound with IngramSpark

THE JOURNEY TO BRING BACK PLAY

NATAŠA ĆEĆEZ-SEKULIĆ

For Irina

Contents

Foreword xi
Introduction xv

1 Childhood Games 1
2 Discovering Belgrade and Myself . . 13
3 Trust 28
4 Learning Independence (While Getting Away With Misbehaving) . . 43
5 High School (1991 – 1995) 63
6 New Normal 89
7 Years of Isolation: Stress and Harm . 112
8 Toxicity and Disconnection . . . 130
9 Somewhere in Between . . . 157
10 Starting Anew 184
11 Beginning to Heal 203

Acknowledgments 217
About the Author 219

Foreword

In spring 2018, I self-published my first book in the Serbian language. Over the next couple of years, I focused on writing stories for my website. I was in the flow of creating and connecting with my inner voice. I committed to writing every day and learned to be comfortable putting my work out there. I posted stories in both Serbian and English.

When I felt ready to publish the same book in English, I had to find someone to do the translation. At first, I thought it would be best to find someone who knew my language and the recent history of the Balkans. I also wanted someone who could take an unbiased approach. As this book is about my life experiences, my reality, I wished to avoid any interventions or interpretations from a second party.

In the spring of 2019, I hired a young woman, Sarah Rengel, whose family is originally from Croatia. She knew the language and society well; she grew up in Australia and studied English literature in Australia and England. We started off with a lot of enthusiasm and successfully passed a number of pages back and forth. Due to our lives in different time zones and many personal and professional tasks and obligations, we didn't make the desired progress.

During the time of COVID-19, while in a process of rethinking and readjusting, I decided to take a new approach. In late 2020, I turned to an editor from Canada, Darcy Nybo. We laid out the plan of our work, and I sent her my text with everything that had been done up until that point.

As expected, Darcy came up with a lot of questions, recommendations, and suggestions. Her valuable feedback made me dig deeper into every paragraph. I created titles for every chapter, I rewrote unclear lines, and added facts and context.

Then I found myself at a crossroads. A big part of me wanted to expand the story because I now saw many gaps. I also had new ideas on how I could write it differently. Over the years, my creative force has been revitalized, and I gained a deeper understanding of my life experience. I became less resistant to exposing some dark moments and more at ease with sharing them with others.

On the other hand, today's Nataša wanted to honour the person she was when she started writing her book in Serbian (*Danas nam je divan dan*[1]) and courageously looked into the abyss. Only she knew how excruciating it was for her to go back. She had to

---

[1] The original, Serbian version of the *Journey to Bring Back Play*, published in 2018.

face her pain, grieve her losses, and stay in a process that dropped her to her knees.

Although that book was the first thing I ever wrote, I don't remember the writing struggles. Instead, I remember huge emotional distress caused by episodes that were popping out from my subconscious without any order, often leaving me clueless about the meaning or goal of my labour. When I'd finished writing my book, I felt like I'd been through years of therapy. I understand now that writing my story helped me work through my trauma and allowed my repressed self-expression to awaken.

I chose to leave the book as it was, so in essence, this English version isn't different from the original, but it also isn't a pure transcription. It complements some parts with more details.

There is also something coincidental with the moment of this book's translation, something I couldn't have anticipated or ever arranged myself, which is worth mentioning here.

For years, in many of my encounters, I struggled to explain to my interlocutors what it was like to be in my teens and experience sudden societal change and the sense of disorientation which comes with it. No matter how hard I tried, no one knew how isolation of one's country can take a toll on one's life. Many didn't understand how it can reshape your identity, shift your worldview, and break your relationships;

how it is tiring and despairing to navigate your young adulthood through uncertainty and constant outside pressure and conflict. Feeling unseen, and in many ways disconnected from the rest of the world, I believed I would carry the weight in silence. Along the way, I learned to keep these experiences to myself and even find peace with that fact.

But in the year 2020, the spread of the deadly coronavirus flipped that state of being forever as it brought the experience of change, fear, isolation, and restrictions to millions of people around the globe. I was unexpectedly put back together with the rest of humanity and able to recognize many who could empathize and directly relate to my life experience.

Because of this, new titles for some chapters such as "New Normal", "Years of Isolation: Stress and Harm" and "Toxicity and Disconnection" have been deliberately used. Today, these titles have become experiences much more familiar and relevant to the world than they were when I wrote my first book in Serbian.

In the end, I can only wish for the resolution of this crisis and hope humans will come out of this experience more compassionate and united. I hope for new solutions to our global-local problems and shared values to guide us, as we create a new world.

Victoria, May 2021.

Introduction

Map of Central/South Europe from the 1980s; countries such as Yugoslavia, Czechoslovakia, and USSR do not exist today.

I was born in Southeast Europe, in the country of Yugoslavia, which existed from 1918 until 1991. For that period, four generations of my family, including me, lived inside its borders. We were all members of the same ethnic group, we spoke the same language, and we passed down similar traditions and customs.

In many other important ways, however, my ancestors and I actually lived in completely different countries. Our societies and cultures, although barely thirty years apart, were shaped by clashing ideologies, mindsets, and values which made us lead unalike lives. If someone were to put us on the same stage, next to each other, I guess we would perceive one another as strangers.

My great-grandfather, for example, spent his adult life living in a kingdom, whereas his grandson, my father, grew up in a republic. At the beginning of the 20th century, religion used to be part of the ruling hand and played an important role in people's everyday lives. Whereas from 1945, when my parents were kids, the country became secular, and religion for many was forbidden or forgotten. As far as I know, my great-grandmother didn't know life outside of her family and closed-off community, but my grandmother was literate and able to make a living on her own as a single mother of two.

Like elsewhere in this world, many of these disparities came out of political shifts, migrations, and global societal movements and breakthroughs. In our case, however, they came out of war. It was always war that destroyed the way of life and tore apart bonds between generations. In a way, every single individual in my family was left to navigate life on their own, dealing with the challenges of bare survival and, at the same time, severe psychological trauma. Except for our last name and genes, I found

INTRODUCTION

war trauma to be that particular fact of life that glued us all together.

Although I wasn't directly exposed to the realities of hostility and brutality of war, I spent my teenage years and young adulthood in its shadow. I saw one reality disappearing in front of my eyes and another emerging from distress, dysfunction, and scarcity. Nothing remained intact.

For a long time, a big part of me was reluctant to accept and integrate many of my life facts, and I lived without realizing how that attitude had affected me. It took more than two decades for me to stop and take a closer look at my life journey.

CHAPTER ONE
Childhood Games

One of my favourite games when I was growing up was The Matches. I would play it with the children from my neighbourhood, always on the same spot, which was right beneath my apartment window. We would usually meet up in the early evenings, when the light from the streetlamps and the apartment block above would give us a little more time to play.

"Number Five! Go! Go!" An elected referee would call upon players while standing halfway between teams. He would watch the players with this number run out from their starting positions and race towards the stick that lay at his feet. Their goal was to grab it as quickly as possible to gain a point for their team.

When I think back on my childhood, I don't remember a single day without a game of some sort. In autumn, when it rained, we would race from room to room, sometimes through the basement or the passageway of our building. We spent our winters on the little hill next to the parking lot. It was small, but as far as we were concerned, it was a perfectly good ski slope. Spring and summer transformed our streets into spacious playgrounds. In one of them we jumped over elastic skipping ropes; in another, we chased after balls. We used a nearby park as a stage for the Eurovision Song Contest,[2] and the parking lot for drawing the outlines of houses where we welcomed imaginary guests.

I never understood when elderly people asked us why we played there.

"It's not safe here," they'd say. They thought those old backyards of theirs were more appropriate places for children's adventures. They would add, "There's concrete everywhere and only two swings for so many children."

They waxed lyrical about things I never noticed. I rushed outside by skipping every second step on the stairs of our building. Every time, it was as though a new adventure from the TV series *Journey to the Centre of the Earth*[3] was about to begin. I always encountered a space full of life, and it was precisely its lack of borders that formed my first impression of the world.

---

2   Known as Eurovision, it is an annual international competition created in 1956. To date, it has showcased over 1,500 songs from 50 different countries.

3   An American cartoon made in the late 60s. A small group of explorers follow the old trail from a cave, hoping to find the lost kingdom of Atlantis at the Earth's core. They are not alone. The evil count and his servant also search for Atlantis and all the power that comes with it. After they seal the entrance to the cave, the explorers start their journey to the centre of the Earth. They come across various underground tribes and creatures and go through a number of adventures.

Everything in it was perfect. As the third child and a twin sister, I always had company. I wasn't afraid of beginnings, nor of kindergarten or of school. Being taken out of my familiar environment never seemed to upset me.

I remembered other people's houses by their smells, by the cakes they baked or by the freedom they granted me. In some, we could shout at the top of our lungs, and nobody would even notice. In others we could ask for anything, all the things we'd never dare to ask for at home, and we'd get them.

The thing that truly made every place unforgettable was always my new playmates. With them, every unfamiliar space would become known and seemed like a second home. I needed time to adjust to the rules of our games, which were somewhat different from what I was used to, but basically, that didn't change much. What mattered the most was that we were together. The energy between us flowed freely, and the end of every day was just a short break, after which we'd continue playing as if we'd never stopped.

These days, I see the same thing in my daughter. If we make a building out of blocks before going to bed and only half-finish it, the first thing she'll say the next morning, before she even asks for a drink of milk, is that we have to carry on. She'll jump out of bed and pick up a building block, placing it where she wants it to go.

"You see, Mommy, how big the building is now," she'll say, continuing with the game.

Whenever I watch or read an interview with someone, I'm always amazed to hear people say they knew ever since they were a child what they wanted to be when they grew up. I don't remember anybody ever asking me that question. Even if they had, I'm sure it would only have confused me. I wasn't aware that I would grow up one day, or that it meant I would have to be something when I did. Carefree and unrestricted as I was, I would probably have said I didn't want to get older, and if I really had to, I would want to keep playing.

I was so passionate about playing that I entered into every game as if it was the only one in the world. For example, I loved four-team dodgeball. Or there could be only two teams. It didn't matter. The point was that I was always assured of a place in that game, and more often than not, I was the captain of my team.

I'd come onto the field when the opposing team started to celebrate their imminent victory. Most of the players already believed there were only a few more moves to make before the end. Most, but not me. I played to exhaustion as I had no intention of easily admitting defeat. I honestly didn't understand my friends who just sat on the sidelines and waited for the game to finish. Who knows, maybe they felt better standing away from the battlefield and keeping their head safe from the ball.

I was one of those who wanted the impossible: to win every time. The lower my odds of winning, the more determined I was. Many times, I emerged triumphant and so, quite logically, I was welcomed in every new match. I knew I would be among the first when teams were picked, and I searched for those who were similar to me. I believed a desire to win could face down even the greatest challenge. Nobody could have convinced me the result was already clear and that my participation in the game wouldn't make much difference.

One day, I asked my twin brother where he was off to. I saw him grab the key to the basement, and I was curious to know why. He was hurriedly putting on his trainers so he could get out of the apartment as fast as possible.

"I'm going to ride my bike." He then mentioned some mutual friends. "We've all got to meet at the parking lot and ride round the neighbourhood once or twice. Maybe today I'll get over all the obstacles without falling," he said excitedly.

"Can I go with you?" I asked, without waiting for an answer. It sounded interesting, so I rushed into the bathroom to get myself ready. I called out for him to wait for me.

"You can't go. It's not for girls," he said.

"Excuse me?" I stopped in my tracks.

"Really, there's not a single one. It's all boys."

My brother never thought about games as being for girls or for boys before, because we always played together. But this time, he distanced himself. When the game involved older kids, he never knew what they would say if I showed up. Our peers knew the two of us came as a set, but the older crowd had its own rules.

"I'm coming, wait for me!" I hollered, as I refused to obey.

We showed up at the parking lot at the appointed time. We couldn't both join the group since we only had one bicycle, but that didn't stop me from discovering what kind of game it was. If I liked it, I figured he could go once, and the next time I'd go.

I saw how some of the boys were looking at me and knew they didn't approve. Yet I didn't care and was more than ready to face them.

My father played an important role in how I looked at myself and life in general. He used to tell me that every person decides how far they'll go in the world. During my childhood, especially if he had a good reason, and at least three times a week, I would hear him say, "Nobody can tell you what your place in life is; you need to find it for yourself!"

As I got older, I never once thought I couldn't do something, or that I wasn't allowed to, because I was a girl. That's why I was very stubborn with anybody who tried to force that cliché on me. No way, I wouldn't follow. I was always ready to stand up for myself or find a way to push back. Luckily for me, there was rarely much complaining. Also, there would often be another girl around who was like me, so I frequently ended up joining in those games more easily than expected.

Looking back on them now, those bike rides were unpredictable and risky adventures, the kind of thing only a child would think up. We'd start out side-by-side on a steep road, and we'd ride down the next street with our hands up. We'd line up at the bottom and go after our chosen leader, who selected ever harder challenges for us. We rode over sand and rocks, our wheels passing through bushes; we went up hills and down again, sometimes aiming for dirty puddles the rain left behind.

Our hearts pounded as if they were about to leap out of our chests, but nobody ever considered giving up. We tirelessly followed one another and approached the finish line as a pack.

Completing the entire course without falling gave us the right to proclaim ourselves the Chosen Ones. Although I was as dirty and scratched up as the rest were, that's exactly how I felt. After the ride, those boys who had doubts about me treated me differently. What was even more important for me was that I confirmed my father was indeed right: it was up to me to find my place in this world.

As a kid, I spent a lot of time on stage, both in kindergarten and later in school. I was picked to recite, sing, dance, or emcee, and I enthusiastically took part in every performance. That said, I never imagined myself as a famous person like someone on TV, nor did I ever understand the keenness with which others discussed celebrities. I watched a lot of movies and TV shows, but it was ordinary people and, more often than not, other children, that left the biggest impressions on me. I admired the ones who had done something worthy of attention and awe, and I wanted to be like them: brave, wise, and helpful.

Nonetheless, there was one exception: a TV show I would have gladly signed up to participate in, if I could have. I used to imagine that by some miracle I'd been chosen to play a part. And just that thought was already excitement enough.

The show was called *Games without Borders*.[4] Teams from various countries competed against one another in a range of tasks that had to be completed without mistakes or within a certain time limit. The game was intense from the very beginning and

---

4   A European television game show that started in France, broadcast from 1965 until 1999. Many European countries took part in this show. Each time, a different city hosted the games. They were typically staged outdoors, close to historic market squares, famous buildings, lakes, or the sea.

demanded each participant be physically prepared, persistent, and agile. Every single move they made was important, as it was crucial for the final score.

We watched these events as if our lives depended on the number of points the contestants received. In my house, between my siblings and me, defeat was unacceptable. I cannot count the times we cried out when our country's team was losing. We leapt up from our armchairs and waved our arms at the opposing team, thinking somehow that would make them fall or make a mistake. With our fingers, we'd draw lines on the TV screen to show our team members where they needed to go. Or we would fall on our knees and pray to the heavens to freeze the countdown on the scoreboard so we'd have enough time to finish the game. When we were winning, though, everything was different. We were overwhelmed with joy. We'd chant *"Ole-ole!"* from the terrace and laugh like crazy. We'd put off going to bed for hours because we were too excited to fall asleep.

The very next day, in our neighbourhood or in Physical Education class, we'd hold our own *Games without Borders*. Ideas flowed from all sides: what we had to squeeze through, what we had to jump over or run around, how many times we had to touch a certain pillar, and how fast we had to bring back a stick to our teammate. There was panic and confusion on the one hand, whistles and cheering on the other.

Everything buzzed with activity like a massive hive, while glimpses of movement and the expressions on others' faces spoke to the endless joy of each moment.

The game exposed the best in us. One person was very good at jumping over hurdles; another knew how to keep their team together and motivate them to persevere. The third could incite mirth because of their clumsiness, which caused us to literally double up on the ground with laughter. There was commotion all around us, and we were so absorbed in the game that we didn't pay attention to the time or know what day it was. We'd be brought back to reality by the ringing of the school bell or the sound of someone's mother calling for her child to come home.

Recently I spoke with my daughter and said, "To become a mature grown-up, you first need to play a lot." She was fighting the idea of starting preschool, and she tried to negotiate with me. She even suggested it would be better if she could start working right away, like Mommy and Daddy. During those moments, I was reminded about that famous question: What do you want to be when you grow up? So, I decided to ask her and then remind her one day what her answer was.

"A snowman!" She surprised me. The first thing that popped into my head was her obsession with Disney's animated film *Frozen*,[5] where she had first seen the snowman Olaf. She was so fascinated by him that she wanted to dress as Olaf for Halloween. Back then, she wasn't old enough to follow the plot of a film, or the characters, or their role in the story, so she didn't choose him for that reason. To some extent, I could understand why she didn't want to be one of the princesses of The Kingdom of Arendelle.[6] They were everywhere. Almost every girl her age was wearing princess gowns, shoes, and tiaras. At every party, there was at least one Elsa or Anna.

My daughter had long hair and liked hair clips and ribbons. She became interested in dresses and begged me to paint her nails. Yet, despite all that strong female energy, she didn't want to be a princess. She wanted to be a snowman.

I wondered why. Perhaps it was because she'd never seen snow, except on television and in children's shows. Even though Canada is famous for its harsh winters, snow is quite rare in the city of Victoria where we live. Here, during the winter, the warm Pacific currents often bring clear skies and days which look more like autumn. Who knows, maybe a sculpture made of snow seemed like something out of a fairy tale to her.

---

5   A 2013 American animated musical fantasy movie made by Walt Disney Studio. Olaf, Anna, and Elsa are the main characters. Princess Anna sets off on a journey to find her sister Elsa, break her sister's icy spell, and save their kingdom from winter's cold grip.

6   The fictional kingdom where Elsa and Anna were born.

Finally, I asked her why she wanted to be a snowman. Without thinking she replied, "Everything Olaf the Snowman does, he does with a smile and a dance."

So, it was about *Frozen*, but it was also about something else. I liked what I heard, and it also made me think a bit. My daughter reminded me of something that is so valuable in this life, but somehow overlooked: it's often the gestures and laughter of the people one loves that hold all the beauty of one's life.

CHAPTER TWO
Discovering Belgrade and Myself

When I was growing up, my parents' apartment was the only address I ever knew. All my relatives, as they used to tell me, had always lived in the same place too. I remember them talking about their homes, and how they were attached to their way of life. This led me to conclude that everybody in the world lived exactly where they wanted and how they wanted.

"I couldn't live without the river below my house, my garden, and my threshing floor," my father's sister said.

"The centre of Belgrade[7] is less than an hour's drive away from us," my mother's family would add. For hundreds of years, they'd been closely tied to the region surrounding the city.

---

7 The capital of the Republic of Serbia. Belgrade had become the capital for the first time in 1403. Because the city was surrounded with high walls made of white stone, it was named Belgrade, meaning White City. It is located in Southeast Europe at the confluence of the Sava and the Danube Rivers.

"Whenever we want, we can come downtown. But here, we have more peace and companions who are like us."

For my parents, Belgrade was the last stop on their journey. In Belgrade, both of them had searched for and found what they'd been missing somewhere else. My mother found a freedom of movement, and my father more life opportunities and the chance to make something of himself. For them, the years that led up to my birth were marked by study, work, sacrifice, and constant moves from one place to another. When they finally settled down, they never even considered relocating again. The desire for change disappeared like an underground stream. It would appear from time to time in some other forms, most often in the demands that settling down and raising a family of five made on them.

Just like my relatives, I had always lived in one place, and I couldn't even imagine another type of existence. If someone had asked me then about life, like any child I would have said that nothing existed before I was born. Well, my parents existed, as did my brother and sister, and somehow lots of other people. But my city, as I saw it, was born with me. I uncovered it bit by bit, accepting everything it contained with open arms. In doing so, it was as though our beings melded together. I felt its pulse and, even today, that identical beat helps me get a sense of other cities.

"I know exactly what you mean," a friend of mine said, when I told her this after returning from a trip to America. I'd been enchanted by New York City.

"It's that familiar roar," I added.

"Yeah, I know. You feel it here." She pointed to the area around her heart.

"Right there," I confirmed. "Some cities you hear first in yourself, and then you see them with your eyes. That's what this city of ours is like."

Belgrade is not a peaceful and reserved city. You don't need to sneak up on it. The bustle of the city constantly draws you in, inviting you to dive deeper into it. I know many people who, encountering it for the first time, were left with a momentary sense of wonder. As I learned, it's mostly because of its rhythm. That sound was for me like a foreign language I somehow already knew. Before I realized what *the words* meant, I understood them because of what they evoked within me.

My most important image of Belgrade is the image of my room. We always called this room the kids' room, even after we'd all grown up. Back then, it looked like many others. There was a bunk bed and another bed off to the side, a desk and a folding chair, and the same ceiling lamp that half the neighbourhood had, but in a different colour. There were also the curtains and paintings my mother picked out.

I wasn't attached to things, as they weren't important to me. It didn't matter whether the beds faced this way or that, if we had wallpaper or the walls were painted, or if we had a carpet instead of a rug. The kids' room went through different phases during my childhood, but what made that room so special was the presence of happiness and excitement. In the blink of an eye, the beds could become ski jumps from which we'd descend onto a mass of pillows we'd laid out on the floor, pretending that we were Matti Nykänen.[8] Or we'd wrap ourselves in blankets and act as if we were our country's bobsled team, competing in the final of the Olympic Games. This was the place where we became doctors, mechanics, or stylists; where we sorted stickers into albums; and where we solved jigsaw puzzles late into the night. This space was just ours, and our parents wouldn't enter it without a reason, especially if we'd got into our beds on time and put all our toys back where they belonged.

We shared it only with our relatives and the children who came to visit us for birthday parties and holidays. During those moments, we couldn't stay still for five minutes. Nothing could prevent us from falling to the ground and leaping up again. Not a single "Be quiet!" could stop the sheer force of our

---

[8] A famous Finnish ski jumper (1963–2019) who won five Winter Olympic medals in the 80s.

laughter, our tumbles, and jumps. I only realized years later how unbearable we must have been, when I saw my downstairs neighbour avoiding eye contact with me. Every time I'd greet her in the hallway, she remained cold. She looked straight through me and never responded in a way other neighbours did. I didn't know why. I understood her much later when I learned about the headaches she suffered because of us.

My "room" quickly stretched to wider areas, which included the space in front of my building, the surrounding parks, the parking lot, the sports fields, and the streets that led to the bus stop and the other side of the neighbourhood. My world expanded quickly, and I explored it freely and with curiosity. Nobody had to encourage me or ask me twice to go out of my comfort zone.

One afternoon, I sat in front of my building waiting for siesta time to finish. I stood by, expecting my friends to come down from their apartments so we could pick up where we'd left off before lunch. Along came a girl my age. She was with her mother.

"Hi, what are you doing here?" she greeted me.

"I'm waiting for someone to come down. Where are you off to?" I could see that she was wearing a special outfit and had a backpack.

"I wanted to start folk-dancing, so Mom's going to sign me up for a dancing group," she told me.

"Folk-dancing? What's that?" I asked innocently. I had no clue what she was talking about.

"It's where you perform with traditional costumes on. Boys and girls dance together while someone plays the accordion," she told me in one breath.

"Do you want to come with us?" her mother offered. "To see what it's like? Maybe you'll like it too."

"I've got to ask my mom," I said. I raced over to the terrace and shouted out. I'd forgotten it was still siesta time. "MO-OM!"

She emerged and shook her head. "Why are you yelling?"

"I've got to ask you something. Can I go with our neighbours," I gestured in their direction, "to folk-dancing? We're going by car, and I'll come back with them."

My mother looked in the direction I'd indicated and greeted our neighbour with a smile. That was all I needed to take off. In the next moment, I was in the car heading off to a place that, until a few moments ago, I hadn't even known existed.

For years, Belgrade persistently and unceasingly knocked on my door. Sometimes it brought huge surprises, sometimes tiny ones, but it always found a way to make me happy. I stored every new experience, every impression deep within me. I still carry them around as a kind of inheritance.

DISCOVERING BELGRADE AND MYSELF

My brother and I went to the Central Cinema in a part of the city called Zemun[9] to watch a film that everybody at the time was talking about: *Ghostbusters*.[10] We stood in a line full of children our age and waited for the doors of the cinema to open. I don't remember who took us on this particular adventure, but my guess is it was Dad, as he would usually go ahead of time to buy tickets for the shows. Because my brother and I were still very young, I'm not sure if we could read all the subtitles displayed on the big screen. I struggled to finish the lines in the second row.

All I can recall is the end of the film. The two of us were up on our feet and dancing to the theme song which, by the way, still makes me sway when I hear it today. For days afterwards, we pretended we were off on a similar expedition. We made special weapons out of the top half of Dad's pyjamas, which we pulled onto one of those long brushes for cleaning ceilings. We tiptoed through the apartment, opened cupboards and doors to rooms, and laughed as we were winning the fight against terrifying ghosts.

---

9   A municipality in western Belgrade with a rich history and various cultural influences: Celtic, Roman, Hungarian, Turkish, Austrian, and Slavic. Until 1934, Zemun was a separate city.

10 A 1984 American supernatural comedy about a group of professors investigating paranormal activities in the city of New York. The film was considered a phenomenon and an example of a cult blockbuster.

I remember standing in the Zeleni Venac[11] neighbourhood, where many bus lines have their last stop, waiting for my younger cousin to come. I wasn't older than thirteen when I invited him to go ice-skating with me. Finally, I was old enough to chaperone someone dear to me on a new adventure. I tossed my skates over my shoulder and threw on a big smile. I wanted everyone to see how proud and happy I was.

We counted the bus stops as we descended along November 29th Street,[12] and at the bottom of it we got off and rushed into The Pioneer Hall.[13] We split into different changing rooms to get ready and then joined the other skaters on the rink. But instead of pirouetting across the ice, as we'd hoped, we spent the entire evening red-faced with shame, falling flat on our faces in front of the youngsters who kept getting in our way.

One-nil for you guys. I promised myself they wouldn't make fun of us next time.

---

11 A famous public market and one of the biggest bus stations in Belgrade.

12 Today called Despot Stefan Boulevard; streets in Serbian cities changed their names a number of times during the turbulent 20th century. Among other things, street names tell the story of a country and society shaped by different ideologies, mindsets, and values.

13 Belgrade's indoor sports arena built in 1973; today called The Aleksandar Nikolić Hall.

The Gardoš neighbourhood,[14] with its little open-air amphitheatre, was the place where I'd meet up with my middle school friends. Gardoš was home to a unique art festival, known as Summer Theatre Stage, which held the best live performances of the year.

Right next to the amphitheatre, there was the famous Gardoš Tower with a small gallery at the bottom and a dizzying spiral staircase which led up to the balcony. We always climbed up those stairs to enjoy the astonishing view. To the left, the wide Danube River[15] stretched for miles, all around, hundreds of roof tops lay before us, and in the distance skyscrapers soared. This tower was built in the 19th century as a memorial to the country and culture that no longer existed, and sometimes, just being around it would transport our minds back in time. We leapt into those past times eagerly, as though we were playing the leads in some good old movie.

Sometimes I'd wander around with my girlfriends and take photos. Other times, I would come to listen to young indie rock bands. Even today, I remember one with particular sentiment. Three boys and one girl, just schoolkids my age, had a band and

---

14 An urban neighbourhood and historical landmark of Zemun. Gardoš is also the name for one of the three manmade hills on which the historical core of Zemun was built.

15 The Danube is the second-longest river in Europe; one of two rivers that flows through Belgrade.

played their own songs. A young music teacher from their school was their mentor and helped them with lyrics and harmonies. He was also their biggest fan and used every chance to encourage them not to give up on their dreams. As I listened to their songs and sang along with them, I felt as though I was soaring over that unseen but ever-present border that adults had set up for us. What a feeling! More than ever before, at least in my mind, I was free of judgements and conditions, and nothing I dared to wish seemed impossible.

In my first year of high school, I had a group of older friends who accepted me despite the difference in our ages. I loved sharing my points of view with them and embraced every opportunity to learn from them and expand my life experiences. One Sunday morning, they invited me to go with them to the Vinyl Record Market at the Student Cultural Centre.[16]

If I am honest, I'd have to admit that I perceived this invitation as a kind of test for my coming-of-age. I was so excited and could hardly wait for the school week to come to its end. I remember my parents being

---

16 Known as SKC, a gathering place for progressive young adults in Yugoslavia and Serbia. Before World War II, this beautiful building in downtown Belgrade was the Officers' House, where many balls and humanitarian events were organized. The building was built in 1895.

surprised when they saw me getting up so early on a weekend. They usually complained because I often got up at a time, they repeatedly said, that was not at all appropriate for a responsible young adult. That Sunday, I lied and said I was going to do something for school, and that this was the only time in the day my schoolmates and I could get together. To play it safe, I went along with anything they asked for. "No worries, on my way back home I will go to the public market and buy the veggies and fruit. Of course, I'll take care of it."

"She's finally come to her senses," I heard behind me, and I rushed off so that I'd arrive in front of Beograđanka[17] at the time we'd agreed upon.

The Vinyl Record Market was the only market where I didn't feel awkward about haggling and trying to get the price I wanted. I liked this game. Sellers offered something which was obviously so precious to them that they weren't in a rush to sell it to just anyone.

First off, they'd ply a customer with questions to see if he or she was ready for this treasure hunt. Even though the buyer wasn't aware of it, the seller knew that a new discovery lay hidden in every song. The words and chords would create a specific atmosphere,

---

17 A building 101m high in downtown Belgrade, opened in 1974. Beograđanka is a symbol of the city, and it translates as Belgrade Lady. This skyscraper currently houses department and retail stores, TV and radio stations, the IKEA head office, and other businesses.

images, or insights which would soon become a part of their personal world.

Every single record was important, and each one had its place in one person's journey. They were like a secret sign, the only genuine reflection of one's inner being. Many generations grew up alongside those records. Sometimes music helped by lifting their spirits; on the other hand, certain lyrics pushed listeners to dive deep into the depths of their souls.

I remember following my friends from one pile of records to another, while listening to every question they asked and soaking in every moment of those exchanges. From one Sunday to another, I let myself be guided in this new direction. Although for many months it remained unfamiliar, at least it wasn't as scary as it seemed at the beginning. And that was crucial for me. I didn't notice the moment when I stepped up into the role of buyer and became comfortable chatting about the things I was still learning.

I was fifteen when I was first introduced to the Belgrade International Film Festival,[18] and had a different encounter with the so-called Seventh Art.[19]

---

18 An annual film festival founded in 1971. It is a pillar event of cultural life in Belgrade. From 2015, it was transformed into an official competition festival.

19 Another term for filmmaking coined by Italian thinker, Ricciotto Canudo. The arts have been classified in this order: painting, architecture, sculpture, literature, music, performing, and filmmaking.

Instead of my regular movie time that usually occurred in the early afternoons with popcorn and juice, this experience was a completely different adventure.

I had friends who'd rush out of morning class so they could make it to the ticket office on time, right before the doors opened. Back then, that was the only way we could secure tickets for the films we wanted to see. We would meet up later in front of the cinema and join the long lines filled with many other film-lovers. I stood in the crowd and paid close attention to the people around me. I recall being especially fascinated with one father, who came to drop off his teenage daughter at the show. He was interested to hear details about the movie plot and its director, and as a fifteen-year old, I thought it was just the coolest thing. I envied the girl who had such an up-to-date role model and wished my father was the same.

That year, at midnight, I went to see Jim Jarmusch's[20] film, *Night on Earth*. I felt like I was taking part in the most exciting event in the city. There were many people in front of the Sava Centre,[21] and most of them could barely wait to enter the cinema.

---

20 An American film director, producer, screenwriter, and musician (1953). *Night on Earth* is a 1991 comedy-drama. It is a collection of five short episodes taking place during the same night in five different cities: Los Angeles, New York, Paris, Rome, and Helsinki.

21 An international business and cultural centre in Belgrade, named after the river Sava. The Centre has been a host to numerous events and performances. Completed in 1979, the building was declared a cultural monument in 2021.

As we approached the front door, a girl grabbed me by the sleeve and got right in my face.

"C'mon, kid, you still have a lot of time ahead of you. Please sell me your ticket. I don't want to miss this moment." I wasn't sure why she was making this so dramatic.

My friends stepped in and pulled me closer, where they could guard me with their bodies. "Don't mind her, just keep moving, we're almost in there."

The hall was completely full. People sat on the floor, in the aisle, and between the seats. The atmosphere was charged with laughter and chatter even while the movie played, but at the end, I swear, I heard something like an explosion. Applause and shouting reverberated through the room as the director of the film climbed onto the stage. The leader of a popular Belgrade rock band accompanied him, which made him even more accepted. When he shared a few words about his work, he did so in a very informal manner and hooked the audience even more. They didn't want to let him leave.

What a sight that was. Even so many years later, without closing my eyes, I can still see it as clearly as if it were happening in front of me now. And I still think it would have made a great postcard, if somebody had captured the scene where the guest receives a long standing ovation from the cheerful crowd. In a time when there were no mobile phones, I took a mental picture of this event without knowing it would be one of my favourite memories of the final decade of the twentieth century.

There are countless similar experiences I could talk about for hours. Many of them I thought I'd forgotten, but just a word or a sound is all it takes to remind me of them. Some encounters are moments when I came to know my hometown better. Others are situations where I discovered my very self.

    I found them to be significant as they touched or awoke something within me, something which led me to a brand-new stage of my life. Even though I didn't know what the future would look like, and many times I struggled to give in, I could never go back to who I was before. Not even if I wanted to. As I uncovered this new face of mine, I also came across worlds that had been, until that point, hidden from me.

CHAPTER THREE
Trust

While I enjoyed discovering the locations and trends of my hometown, it was the people who were the reason I was so deeply attached to it. From an early age, I experienced Belgrade as a home to simple and trustworthy people. I divided them all up into two groups: those that came into our home because they were family or friends, and all the others.

I didn't view these other people with distrust or prejudice, but they didn't interest me much. I wasn't one of those children who spent their time with grown-ups. Quite the contrary, I was often uncomfortable in their presence. After greeting them or being introduced to them, I eagerly awaited my parents' permission to run off to my room or hurry down the stairs into a world I called my own.

There were some tiny details that, at the time, I didn't think were particularly important. Later, when the relationships between those closest to me changed, I recalled them as details from another world which I associated with peace and innocence.

Like most of the families we knew, we went on summer vacations and visited our relatives every year. Those moments were preceded by the end of the school year. We got our school reports, thoroughly cleaned our room and desks, and prepared our books for the coming year. This tidy-up was something my parents insisted on as soon as the school year was over. They also expected us to help with a major clean-up of our apartment, which we did without complaint. On our day of departure, when the suitcases were shut and piled up on the rooftop of our car, my parents sat down in the living room with their cups of coffee. They would go through the checklist, marking the boxes and confirming everything was in place: things packed, payments made, relatives informed, and so on. Dad ensured the water valves were turned off, as well as the circuit breakers in the fuse box above our front door, while Mom lowered the shutters and took out the spare keys to the apartment. She entrusted them to our closest neighbours, who lived right next door to us and with whom we shared the wall in our entryway.

Interestingly enough, they weren't part of the group of family friends that regularly visited us, but there was not a single moment of doubt whether or not we would trust them with the keys to our apartment.

"If, God forbid, something happens, use them! If you need us for anything, here's the phone number where you can reach us," my mom said as she thanked them in advance. Nothing ever happened, but every year we re-enacted the same scene. It was entirely normal for your next door neighbour to collect your mail, water your plants, and air out your apartment while you were away.

Closeness between people was a part of everyday life. Some of our female neighbours would simply knock, open the door, and walk into our kitchen. They would sit down with my mother for a smoke break. They'd also bring my father an iron to be fixed, or ask him, if he could, to buy them some vegetables when he went to the market. With coffee cups in their hands, the conversation would stretch out and go into private details, leaving me thinking that nobody kept secrets from one another.

I remember one day when my neighbour gave me a lecture in front of my apartment. Somehow, I hadn't locked the door properly, and she'd come across it while it was hanging wide open. She went in to check if anything had happened and realized that somebody had just been careless.

She saw me at the playground and called out to me from the terrace to come upstairs. She was criticizing me in a calm but stern tone, not for my carelessness, but because while she was scanning the apartment, she'd noticed the beds weren't made.

"Doesn't your mother have enough to do? Now when she gets home, she'll find those beds waiting for her." I received her words as I would from any other adult in my family. I promised I would do it right away. For months afterwards, because I felt ashamed, I avoided her at every opportunity.

In my country back then, it was common to call adults by their first name, in front of which we'd simply add the word "Uncle" or "Auntie." For example, my first neighbour was always Uncle Stevan and his wife Auntie Dušica. I rarely called anyone Sir, Mister or Missus before I reached my teenage years. I saw many people on a regular basis, in banks, grocery shops, hair salons or rec centres, and to me they were less close than a relative, but more than just fellow citizens.

Every now and then, one of those uncles would come to our apartment and talk to my parents about anything that was happening in our community. I got used to him, but then he suddenly stopped coming. We lost touch when he moved to a new address and got employment in another part of town, but I never forgot him. One day, during the 1990s, I ran across him in the middle of a street in my neighbourhood. My friend and I were rushing out from my apartment to the nearest bus stop. We planned to meet with other friends in a café in downtown Belgrade.

Out of nowhere, I saw a familiar face in a group of people passing by. Without saying a word to my friend, I stopped.

"Good afternoon," I said, nodding respectfully. "I am so glad to see you. How are you?" I wondered for a moment if he knew who I was. He stood for a few seconds and then replied.

"Hey, sweetie!" He smiled as broadly as he could while his eyes checked every detail on my face. "Look at you! I barely recognized you! And how are you?"

In the next few minutes, I shared details of my life while he listened.

"You're already in high school? Oh, that's great! And how's your grandmother?" He continued on, going through a list of things people would probably consider private: names, addresses, workplaces.

I told him about the many changes the 1990s brought to my extended family. Some members were displaced and lived as refugees; others remained in their houses, but got laid off and had to struggle to make a living. I switched the topic to change the tone of our conversation.

"Just so you know, my close family has grown since the last time we spoke. It's now six of us." I proudly mentioned the fact that half the neighbourhood knew us because of the dog we had rescued from the street.

"You wouldn't last long if you ended up on her territory!" we joked.

I wasn't even looking in the direction of the bus stop anymore, because I knew we had missed the bus. And I couldn't care less.

There'd always be another bus, but not a moment like this. I knew that for a fact. In the years filled with worry and separateness, there wasn't anything I craved more than to look at a human face and feel seen and connected. His round, kind-hearted face, his familiar, smiling eyes, and the friendly tone were like a medicine for my restless soul.

My friend watched and listened to this whole encounter. She'd met so many people from my extended family, and listened to stories about those she'd never seen, but she didn't know where to place this man.

"Who's that?" she asked after we got on a bus.

"He introduced himself, don't you remember?"

"Yes, I heard his name, but who is he to you?" She looked at me, waiting for an answer.

"When I was a kid, he was our mail carrier!" I could see images of old days running through my head. In one of them, he stood in our hallway and my parents insisted he accept their invitation to stay for a cup of coffee or maybe a glass of beer.

"Dad would always leave me money, so I could pay the phone bill directly to the mail carrier. Back then, we didn't have to go to the post office.[22] I was proud when I learned how to say he should round up the amount or keep the change. Only grown-ups did that."

---

22 In Yugoslavia, as well as in Serbia, utility companies are government-owned, so people can pay their bills either in post offices or banks.

I couldn't stop the words from rushing out from my mouth. "He was always friendly; he always had a smile on his face." I carried on saying whatever came to my mind. I could hardly wait to get back home and share this news with my family.

Back in the 1980s, when parents would pick up their children from school or after an excursion, never once did they fail to ask whether I wanted to go home with them. In the local shop, when I didn't have enough money for the groceries, the owner would send me home with a full bag and always believed I'd be back in a flash with the rest of money. Many times, I left the keys of my apartment under the doormat, because I couldn't be bothered to wait for my brother to come back from the playground. It wasn't a big deal, I thought; nobody would look for them there. And even if they did, so what?

At least three times a year, schoolkids were allowed to knock on every door in the neighbourhood and collect old newspapers. This was a famous school fundraiser in my city we called "Working Saturdays." Our elementary schools would organize students to bring paper to schools in the morning, and later on, the school would pack the paper and take it to the local paper factory. My friends and I would take trollies from the local supermarket and go in groups from building to building. We rang the doorbells, sometimes several times at the same address. We did it even during siesta time, but nobody ever raised their voice to us. My neighbours opened their front doors in their undershirts, with newspapers tucked under their arms. Women answered with curlers in their hair or wooden spoons in their hands.

Back then, I experienced the world as a safe place. All around me, I saw an order that I could easily understand and accept. Everyone had their responsibilities, both youngsters and adults. I remember that in the winter my father would meet up with neighbours from the second floor at an appointed time and shovel the snow from the area in front of the building. They'd clean it one day, our neighbours from the third floor would do the next day, and so on. Nobody disobeyed or ignored a call for help. I'd hear them say, "This is our doorstep, these are our children, our responsibility."

Every Saturday morning, kids had work to do too. We cleaned the pavement, rushed up and down the stairs in search of trash, reported on the lights that didn't work, wiped the glass on the front door, and worked on the flowerbeds in front of the building. We were taught to rely on one another and we counted on each other.

For a long time, I thought this kind of intimacy between people was unique to the place where I'd grown up. People from my country love to say that Serbs have a special way of nurturing and valuing relationships. But I've come to realize this isn't the case. Many of the people I've met, both in Europe and in North America, tell the same story. Humans survived so many challenges throughout the centuries because they stuck together. As we all know, people feel stronger when they know they have somebody to lean on, particularly if that somebody is their neighbour.

A lady I met in a park in Victoria[23] told me she never used to lock the door of her house or car when she was younger. People trusted one another, and it didn't matter who went to pick up or drop off the neighbourhood kids at school. It was only later, she mentioned, about thirty years ago, that people began to distance themselves and became more and more suspicious.

It seems that a new world, a new order, sprouted up across the entire planet and divided people into groups. In every corner of the world, in every community, you can find or hear about the "us and them."

Trust seems to be one of my hardest life lessons and a wound I have to heal. When my husband and I started talking about preschool, trust issues came to the surface and shook up our everyday lives. Just as I thought we'd survived the hardest part, that I'd be able to relax a little now that my daughter was walking and talking, this change came along.

---

23 The capital city of the western Canadian province of British Columbia. Victoria is located on the southern tip of Vancouver Island, and is widely known as the Garden City.

I knew she was ready for preschool. I saw it in the way she interacted with other children in the park or followed what they were doing. She mimicked them and was highly motivated to join in, despite not being able to understand the language. But when she started preschool, she would keep one eye on me and reacted if I was about to go. Every morning, when I dropped her off, she'd tell me to hang on. She was unsure whether she wanted to be with me or stay with the kids.

I knew how she felt as I was sitting on a seesaw too. Part of me wanted her to stay close, where I would do everything to make her safe. And the other part kept withdrawing and encouraging her to explore the world on her own. Like all of us, I knew she also needed a stimulating environment in order to grow.

When I left her, I felt overwhelmed with emotions of fear, guilt, and helplessness. Many times, I cried and did everything I knew would bring about relaxation and a sense of peace.

"She is safe, she is loved," I repeated over and over until I believed it. I had to. That's why I would wipe away my tears, breathe deep, and sometimes pray for her well-being.

I grew up in a circle of trust, which made me a person who believed reliance was a pledge of love and joy, and if given or earned, created wonder. In both my close and extended families, I never felt like a stranger. I spent a part of my winter and summer holidays with my relatives, far away from the eyes of my parents. I considered my uncle's house (my mother's brother) and my aunt's house (my father's sister) my own and had strong emotional attachments to them both.

My grandmother lived with my uncle's family. She would make up to five different breakfasts to satisfy the wishes of all her little grandchildren. Everybody in town knew my maternal uncle and aunt, and we always received tickets for the swimming pool, comic books from a family friend at the kiosk, invitations to try out bowling, trips to the ice cream parlour or to the fair, or visits to our extended family. I treated my two little cousins the same as my actual brother. We shared everything, slept in the same room, had the same friends, played with the same toys, and sat next to each other at family celebrations.

My uncle was a gentle and caring soul. He would stand up for us even when we ran amok. Somehow, in his presence, we were always allowed to push the boundaries and ask for more. I remember once we were all at a family wedding and he took us across the street to get *tulumba*, a sweet pastry, from the bakery. When we returned with our sweets, my parents and aunt were angry out of their minds.

"Where did you get them? And why?" They were mad at him, and even more at us. "How do you dare ask for more treats with all the cakes and pastries you have here?" They questioned our behaviour as they threatened us with a wagging finger over my uncle's shoulder.

"Look, the kids wanted *tulumba* and I said okay," he explained, defending us. "They're just kids. Leave them be!" He sent the adults away while shielding us from their angry looks and lectures.

My father's family lived hundreds of kilometres away from Belgrade. We saw them less frequently, only once a year, but that might be the reason why every visit was accompanied by a great deal of excitement. Sometimes we went by car, all five of us, and sometimes Dad would take me and my brother by train.

I loved approaching the small village on a hill from a distance. A familiar sight greeted us: my aunt's large house; the orchard, garden, and threshing floor with a stable; and my uncle's workshop. My male relatives worked in town and also had a large farm they had to manage. As I was there during summers, I watched hay being mowed with a scythe and made into haystacks. I learned how to stack firewood for the winter or squash plums with my feet for the brandy they made every year. I tried veggies I didn't like, and mulberries, which I knew little about. I also enjoyed watching my aunt knead dough and stretch it out to make those delicious pies of hers. At her side, I made my first contact with farm animals and started taking care of them myself.

As soon as we'd arrive, word would spread in a matter of moments. Our cousins would pull us away to their backyards to play or take us to the river to swim and fish. They also accompanied me to collect water from the springs that flowed from the rocks.

To this day, the whistle of a train, the feel of ferns beneath my feet, the sight of fireflies in the dead of night, and the smell of freshly cut grass can instantly transport me to that place of peace and wonder. A place that now exists only in my memory.

I will never forget the moment I got a key on a large elastic band to wear around my neck. It was a few months before school. I was six years old, but with this responsibility I felt I was now a big girl. When I started school at the age of seven, I learned how to warm up my lunch and turn on the washing machine. As soon as I started writing, I'd ask my father to let me fill out a payment form to pay the household bills at the bank. There wasn't a shred of doubt in his mind that I could indeed do these things properly.

The same happened in school. My teachers also trusted me with various roles in class, at school competitions, and at performances. Sometimes I was to dance or sing. Other times I had to lead the programme or get in front of the school principal and salute in the name of all the fourth-grade members of the Boško Buha[24] Pioneer Squad.[25] That felt scary, but by taking part in these activities, I learned to deal with pressure. With the help of my mentors, I welcomed new opportunities and, with every rise and fall, I took a step forward.

It was easy for me to assume life wasn't the ruthless struggle we learned about in school or saw in films. I believed all those terrible things were now part of a history class and left far behind in an age before I was born. I was part of a peaceful world, and I welcomed every new day with the conviction that it would be full of wonderful moments. I acted as though I knew the secret to eternal happiness, because I felt as if I was somehow always in the right place at the right time.

I was still a child, but I couldn't wait to be a teenager. "Imagine what it's going to be like when we're eighteen," I'd tell my brother.

I was enthusiastic about the idea that my eighteenth birthday would get me more freedom and unveil all the curtains of the big and amazing world. I daydreamed about that future moment coming and bringing fulfilment and joy.

---

24 A young Yugoslav partisan (1926–1943), who fought and died in World War II.

25 In former Yugoslavia, all elementary students of one school were members of one Pioneer squad. Students actively participated in different educational, cultural, sport, and leisure activities. On special occasions pioneers wore uniforms: dark blue pants or skirts, white shirts, red scarves, blue caps with a badge.

I recall once standing in the middle of the street in my neighbourhood and looking into the future with my eyes wide open. Completely enthralled as though I was in a fever, I whispered, "I can hardly wait for you."

CHAPTER FOUR
Learning Independence (While Getting Away With Misbehaving)

"What's going to happen when I'm not around anymore? Who's going to live and speak up for you?" These were the words I heard often from my parents.

Independence, both of mind and action, was the first lesson they insisted on, particularly my father. Whenever I'd ask him to come outside on the playground and resolve some issue on my behalf, he responded by asking those questions.

Having three kids must have been a huge duty and responsibility. While my parents may have managed to provide everything we needed, they didn't think we needed them to do everything for us. I realized later they actually gave us more freedom than most parents did back in those days. For example, they never interfered in my choices of games, friends, or hobbies. I was permitted to enrol in any school or activity I desired. They let me make my own choices and face my strengths and my shortcomings, which made me a person who could think and fight for herself.

Because of my determination, I was loved by many, both as a child and later in life; but this quality, more than any other, was also what distanced me from others. Ironically, the independence I enjoyed despite my age and life experience later became something I bitterly resented my parents for.

I used to say, "How could you even imagine that a normal person could walk around in this jungle of the human race and stay alive?" During young adulthood, I missed having someone to guide me and support me through the rough times.

"It was a different world back then," they said, defending themselves.

My mother told me a story about a time when I was five or six. I don't recall this event, but I do remember her telling it many times. My father had come up with an excellent plan (at least that's how it seemed to him) to teach us how to find our way around an unfamiliar part of the city. He and Mom wouldn't always be there for us, and we'd have to be prepared to deal with the situation. For days beforehand, he rehearsed with my brother and me and made sure we memorized our full names, our home address, phone number, and the bus line that would take us to our neighbourhood. The bus is something that every city kid got used to very early on. You had to know the bus routes, how to validate your ticket, how to ask somebody for directions if necessary, and so on.

The plan was simple. Dad took us to a public market downtown, and after some time, when we weren't looking, he'd step back. He watched from nearby to see how we were getting on, how we behaved along the way, whether we stopped anyone (and if so, who), which direction we took.

He'd follow us from a safe distance, wait until we got on the bus, and then find us, apparently by surprise, wondering how we'd managed to disappear. He'd been happy beyond words when he'd come home and confide in my mother that we'd dealt with the situation without any drama. He told her we held hands, looked around, lifted up our heads and, without catching sight of him, headed off in the direction of the bus that led us back home.

I learned to find my way around Belgrade on my own very early on. There's one story I love to retell. One summer, after finishing first grade, I went to a summer camp by the seaside with my schoolmates. I liked those camps, and I continued going for years after, but I also enjoyed the time preparing for the trip. Mom and I would usually go to one of the department stores downtown and buy things I needed. I loved those shopping trips, and I wouldn't have missed them for anything in the world. We'd go up from the ground floor to the third and decide on everything together: flip-flops, towels, swimsuits, and beach mats.

Mom would always pick up some things that belonged on her private list of household goods, things Dad didn't always know about. In those stores we had our pants shortened, curtains hemmed, batteries changed on the wall-clocks, and all sorts of other useful things I thought were fascinating. After the shopping, the two of us would treat ourselves to an ice cream. "Should I buy my favourite vanilla ice cream or maybe chocolate is better?" I always struggled to decide. I would carry the full shopping bags with the biggest smile, knowing that there were only a few days left before I would pack my suitcase and be off to the coast.

But that year, before setting out on this adventure, I faced the prospect of a bus ride I would have to survive on my own. My mother worked downtown, and she didn't want to come home, spend an hour, and then go back there to shop. So she asked me to leave the shopping to her this time. After all, I was only seven and a half, and she didn't expect me to take a bus on my own. I could have said yes, but I didn't want to. Therefore, we agreed that she'd wait for me in the Terazije Square.[26]

---

26 One of the oldest city squares in Belgrade, surrounded by public buildings, cultural institutions, hotels, and parks. Its name was given by the Turks, and refers to the tall water towers built to help transport water to surrounding neighbourhoods. Today, Terazije Fountain is a famous meeting place for Belgrade residents.

I stepped onto the bus and stood right next to the driver. From that position, I watched where we were going, and I was sure I would know where I had to get off. At first, the driver said nothing. He would lean over me to check the passengers in his side mirror and confirm if he could close the doors.

A short time later, however, he asked me, "Say, kiddo, why are you standing by the doors? Tell me, where are you going?"

"My mom's waiting for me at the bus stop at Terazije Square," I said. I was frightened because I didn't speak to older people and especially strangers just like that.

"You've got time. Why don't you find a spot and sit?"

"I'm scared I'll miss my stop, Uncle." I stood in the same place and glanced from him to the floor.

"How about this," he waved towards a double seat next to the front doors. "You sit there, and I'll make sure you get off where you need to. Okay?"

I nodded, turned around, and did what he proposed. I sat in that seat even when people tried to get me to stand up.

"Find your seat somewhere else," the bus driver told them. "I'm responsible for that kid. She has to stay there." Without a word, people would turn their heads and search for a new spot.

When we came to my bus stop, he pointed to the Terazije Square and waved me off as he would to his own child. I ran towards my mother and told her it wasn't at all scary to be alone on the bus. Somehow, I concluded, there are people who will help you, even when you don't ask them to.

My brother and I repeated this independence lesson when we started going to a foreign language school. At ten years old, we discovered another part of the city, one we rarely visited. The only thing we had to do after class was to phone our mother or father and let them know we'd arrived home safely. During the elementary school years, I also went by myself to doctor's appointments, to the dentist, to strengthening exercises in local health units, or to see the hairdresser.

At the age of fifteen, my father had an ID card made for me. As soon as I was legally allowed to, he gave me permission to use his cheques. He thought I wasn't a kid anymore, so why wouldn't I be able to buy clothes and shoes for myself? I appreciated that. If I needed something, I'd let him know my plans. I always carried a telephone card, and I usually used the public phones on Knez-Mihailova Street,[27] in the underpass at the Palace Albanija,[28] or those at the bus station at Zeleni Venac. I'd dial our home number and wait for

---

27 The main pedestrian and shopping zone in Belgrade. This kilometre-long street was named after the Serbian Prince Mihajlo Obrenović. It features a number of important buildings including bookstores, galleries, cultural centres, the main city library, hotels, restaurants etc.

28 When completed in 1939, it was the first skyscraper in southeast Europe, a symbol of Belgrade's economic growth between two world wars. However, people protested its creation, as this location was home to a well-liked bistro with the first public city clock in front of it.

LEARNING INDEPENDENCE

Dad to check his bank balance, after which he would confirm whether I was allowed to spend the money or had to wait until the end of the month.

The state of independence wasn't always clear to me. Sometimes I was confused, and I struggled with its conflicted messages. On the one hand, I felt comfortable being on my own, and I liked being trusted. But on the other, I couldn't often understand the purpose of so many boundaries. I was thirteen or fourteen when I had to answer frequent questions like: "Where are you going, with whom, and when are you coming home?" There were also rules such as if I wasn't home by ten, there would be consequences.

I had to do a lot of convincing and make a lot of promises to persuade my parents to let me go out. Once, they even asked me for a written list of names and phone numbers of the friends I was going out with.

One of my school friends used to justify her parent's behaviour: "It's easier for yours than mine," she said to me one day at the school playground. "Your parents have a spare."

"How can you say that?" I snapped. Even though she was older, she had to be home earlier than me. She was an only child, and her parents followed her every move.

But she was right in one way. I was indeed blessed with an older sister. Some of my friends had older siblings too, and for us it was easier to get our parents to say yes. They felt calmer, knowing that we'd look after one another.

I was only thirteen when I went to my first concert at the Belgrade Youth Centre. Boy, it was an experience I would remember for so long! I found a spot in a corner near the stage, where many people crammed together jumping and singing at once. At one point, during the commotion, some people from the first rows fell on the ones behind them. I was among those who ended up on the floor, in the dark. For some reason, I didn't panic. Maybe because my sister was next to me or because it took me only a few seconds to get back to my feet and continue to jump. While I knew some people who afterwards would avoid concerts or the space next to the stage, I found this situation to be very helpful later on. I had learned how to handle myself in a crowd. That night wasn't a disaster at all. I sang out loud the whole time as I melted into the mass of people I shared the space with.

Within a few months, I opened the door to some of Belgrade's youth clubs. I went to many indoor and outdoor concerts, spontaneous jam sessions on the street, and home parties. Practically overnight, I discovered a world that communicated through magazines, vinyl records, and cassettes. There was a whole range of theme nights, parties, and birthdays as excuses to get together, chat, and sing to our heart's content. Every weekend, our group would break up after midnight, and we'd hurry home on the night buses, which would take us to our neighbourhoods.

I found my close group in girlfriends who were interested in the same things as me. Some were a little older than I was, but I also got on well with my peers who shared similar experiences. Two other girls from my 8th grade class also went out frequently, and we'd exchange and compare our experiences. They were writing a book and used people they knew for their characters. They incorporated real situations they'd been through, playing with dialogues, scenes, and endings. I was one of their heroines, and we laughed about plot twists as we went to and from school.

"Just so you know, you dumped that guy and now you're alone," one of them said to me. The night before, she'd been adding new pages to the story.

"Okay, what am I going to do now?" I asked.

"I am giving you time and space to explore new options," she said.

"All right. I am in," I replied. I could already relate to my character. My days were all about new possibilities, too.

My close group was comprised of four girls from my school, and we spent every spare moment together. We listened to the same music, watched the same movies, exchanged clothes, and looked for ways to entertain ourselves. And that could be anything. We'd go to the riverbank, to the Gardoš neighbourhood, and sometimes downtown to sit in front of the Philosophy department building and observe the older teenagers we admired so much. Over the weekend, if one of us had parents who had gone to a holiday vacation home, we watched VHS tapes, listened to live concerts, and pretended we were already high schoolers.

In the late 1980s, Radio and Television of Serbia expanded and started broadcasting what was known as Channel Three. It was all about the youth and therefore very different from the other two channels. It brought a fun, party-like atmosphere, and had creative young people as speakers. They would start conversations that teenagers and young adults could easily relate to. They also made some silly fake commercials, which were nothing but jokes; these immediately grabbed our attention.

While watching the program together one evening, we got an idea to make our own joke. We became on-scene reporters for a day. It took us a day to set up a plan for this adventure, and one of my three girlfriends had an old camera at home. Her parents kept it as a memento of good old times, although they didn't use it anymore. It made a specific sound, as though a tape was inside. This was just what we needed to assure our interviewees that the recording was real. We found a microphone, thought up some questions, and visited one of the city's public markets.

We kept a watchful eye on local streets to ensure nobody would recognize us and, God forbid, report to our parents. People didn't figure out we were tricksters. Some pushed one another to get first in line in front of our camera and answer a question we asked. It might have been about the weather forecasts or daily price hikes on groceries but, as it would appear, our questions were good enough to show people's personalities and points of view.

We played this game for less than an hour and then put our camera down. We assured people the recording would be released on Channel Three that very evening, so they could prepare to watch it. But minutes after, hidden in the entryway of a local building, we were choking with laughter. "Were we that good or was this luck?" We weren't sure.

We had a lot of fun, nobody caught us, but we never repeated this adventure again. The next week we were onto some other activities, and I let it slip from my memory. I was now inspired by the teenagers only a little older than me, who wrote for magazines or played in bands. I honestly didn't take those episodes too seriously, as I was still so young. I was neither thinking about the future nor what I would like to do one day. But I kept my eyes open and paid attention to the people who knew. Big stories, cover pages, money, and fame weren't of any interest to me. The most important thing of all was to find the group where I felt I belonged.

I was lucky enough to be accepted by my sister's classmates, as well as the older sisters and brothers of my peers. Back then, at the time of my middle school, it meant so much to me to be welcomed into their company.

My older sister was my idol for some time, but our relationship was always tense. She would say things like, "Those are my jeans!" or "You can't wear these shoes." Sometimes, when we'd go out together, she would warn me not to speak to her in public or let anyone know we were related. She didn't want to be seen hanging around with a kid, so she kept creating distance between us, as though I was aeons younger than her instead of less than three years.

Funnily enough, this didn't bother me. I didn't stop peeking into her high school books and was always on high alert whenever she was around. I soaked up every little piece of information she dropped, and later I'd learn everything I could about whatever she'd mentioned. At fourteen, I wanted to look like her, and I begged my mother to buy me the same shoes she wore. Many days, I waited for the moment she headed off to school, so I could "borrow" her jacket or her handbag and show them off as if they were mine.

To stay in my sister's favour, I did many things. For example, I would meet her after school and take

LEARNING INDEPENDENCE

her schoolbag home, so she could stay downtown and spend time with her friends.

One spring, a famous city band, Ekatarina Velika,[29] played at the Belgrade Youth Centre a few days in a row. I'd been to only one of their concerts and had a great time. I wanted so much to go to another, but I hesitated to bring up the topic. I thought I'd be perceived as pushy or ungrateful, so I kept quiet.

My sister, on the other hand, bought a ticket to another concert and planned to go with her schoolmate. They both needed help.

"Can you come tomorrow," she asked me in the evening, "so you and my friend's younger sister can look after our bags?" That younger sister and I were the same age.

"No problem," I replied. "When do I have to be there?" I asked with a smile. I couldn't hide how thrilled I was.

We all met in front of the centre around half past eight, where a mass of young people waited for the doors to open. I enjoyed being a part of this crowd and followed with interest what they were doing or talking about. Some older girls mostly commented on guys, which I didn't consider interesting at that time.

---

29 A rock band from Belgrade considered one of the most influential acts of the former Yugoslav rock scene. From 1982 to 1994, the band made seven studio albums. It ceased to exist after the premature death of the frontman, Milan Mladenović. The band is loved and adored to this day.

I met my sister's classmates, some of whom I knew from her stories. I finally met them in person and felt good when they were nice to me. Every one of them approached to see and say hi to the two cute little sisters.

Of course, they could have acted this way because they had a reason. They needed us, as we were supposed to take care of their bags, too.

The concert started a little later than expected. My friend and I stood up by the fence, near the entrance, keeping an eye on six coats and bags. We danced and sang to ourselves for about twenty minutes. After the third song, my friend had an idea.

"You know what?" she exclaimed. "I'm not going to miss out on this."

"What do you mean?" I was confused. "What choice do we have?"

"Let's have a look in our sisters' bags. Maybe they've got some cash!"

"Man, you're crazy," I protested. "If we do that, we're done."

"Don't worry." She was chilled. "I'll ask my parents to lend me some money, and we'll give it back to them tomorrow," she assured me. "Just go and see if there are any black-market tickets left."

Before I knew it, we were taking the steps down to the basement. With three jackets and three bags on our shoulders, we looked more like we were going camping, not to a concert. We dashed into the hall and jumped up and down as if we'd just been let off a leash. In a single second, I forgot my shenanigans and gave in to the moment.

Gosh, it was so hot in the hall. We could barely breathe from all the heat and the smoke of cigarettes, but we didn't complain. Music lifted us up, and we sang right up until the end, loving every minute of it.

As soon as the band said their goodbyes to the crowd, we ran back to our old spot and acted as if we were innocent. "You're so sweet, maybe we'll see you again," their friends told us. We didn't dare to meet their eyes.

I couldn't keep my mouth shut for even ten minutes. I was so euphoric that I gave us away by the time we got to the second traffic light. I was describing the crowd's reaction to one of the songs, when I heard my sister asking:

"And how do you know that?"

"Oh, damn!" I grumbled. Those six words sobered me up like a cold shower. They found out what we did. A wonderful night ended with a lecture and the promise this was the last time they'd ever rely on us.

Luckily, in a couple of weeks, they forgot about everything. A new chance for a night out appeared, and my sister and her friend needed an accomplice to help them.

I was always there for my sister. I covered for her whenever I could. I protected her as though I was defending myself. Because we were always stepping up and fighting our parents together, we often got the same punishments. When she was grounded, I wasn't allowed to go out either.

One particular occasion has stuck with me forever, and not just because of the punishment. I waited for my sister after school on a Friday night, in front of the theatre. She was going to a concert in the Student Cultural Centre's Garden with her friends. I don't remember who they were or who was playing that night; all I recall was meeting her at the tram stop where I took her school bag. We exchanged a few words and details.

"When Mom and Dad ask, tell them I'm at the theatre with my class. Maybe they won't ask too much this time." She sounded unusually relaxed.

"No worries. I'll wait for you to come back." I was jealous that she was going somewhere I wasn't.

I went home, and when Mom noticed I had my sister's bag, I repeated the story. "She is at the theatre; actually the whole school is there. The theatre made a play out of some book on their required reading list, so it is all being counted as an extracurricular activity." Back in the 1980s, in my country, it wasn't unusual for students to visit theatres and watch a play about the book they had read in language classes.

I was sure my mom wouldn't suspect, and she didn't. She was actually pretty calm and didn't say anything, just looked at the clock. It was still early.

Between 10:00 and 10:30 pm, my dad picked up the clock and wound it up as he walked down the hallway to his bedroom to sleep.

Yes! One down, I thought to myself. I pretended to toy with some cassettes and not follow what was going on in the living room.

It was 11:30 pm when I sensed a change in the atmosphere. Mom was showing signs of worry. She lit cigarette after cigarette and started asking questions. She demanded to know where my sister was.

"Oh, I'm sure she'll be here in a second; she must have missed the bus talking with her friends. It's Friday after all, so she's not in a hurry to come back home." I thought I was being clever. But then again, I was getting nervous and was aware I was slowly using up my last moments before the drama.

"She'll hear me this time when she gets back!" Mom was furious.

Around midnight, Mom was so frightened she said she would wake up my father. I begged her not to. Although I was resisting the temptation to give my sister away, I knew this was the moment I had to tell the truth. I admitted she was at a concert.

I woke up my brother, and we went to wait for the night bus. It was very dark and creepy outside. We hid in the entranceway to a small building where we waited and waited. But my sister didn't appear. My brother went home with the news and went back to bed. I stayed and waited for the next bus. I couldn't go home; I was involved in this mess and partly to blame. Since childhood, the rule in my house was that we were always all to blame, either because you did something or because you could, but didn't. Collective blame was something I felt very early on. For years, I tried to drag myself out from under this kind of sentencing, but with no success.

At last, she appeared on the second bus. I ran out of the darkness and joined her and some neighbours.

"Where have you been?" She looked at me and sensed some danger. I said nothing as I stayed quiet in front of her acquaintances and listened to their impressions from the concert. As soon as we were alone, I told her. "We are in trouble. Mom knows."

Mom waited for us in front of our building. We could see the glow of her cigarette from several dozen metres away. When we approached her, my sister was not even trying to explain the situation. It was useless. Just by the look on Mom's face, you could tell she was mad. She raised her finger and hissed through her teeth that from tomorrow onwards, things would be different in our house. She couldn't yell because it was late and the entire building was asleep.

LEARNING INDEPENDENCE

However, as soon as we got inside our apartment, she loudly and confidently began the process of imprisonment. The first step was to get the house keys back from my sister. She then listed off our punishments.

"Home by nine!" I thought that wasn't too bad, and I kept my mouth shut. "No phone calls!" It then became clearer and clearer to me we'd lose all our hard-earned benefits.

Mom would tell Dad, and it could mean only one thing. He'd cut off all communication we had with our friends. In those days, my dad would often put a padlock on the dial to stop us from using the rotary phone. In my country at that time, we were charged by the minute even for local calls, and he would stare at the phone bill in shock. His idea of making a call was quite different than ours. "All you need a phone for is to say 'Hi, it's me, let's meet there at...' " He couldn't understand why our conversations lasted an hour or even more. "After you set up a meeting, get out and talk face to face."

The two of us hurried off to get ready for bed. We didn't exchange any words. With our heads bowed, we just glanced through our lashes. Mom came into the room and promised this was the last time we decided to do something without checking with them first. She would ensure we would behave from now on.

When we finally got settled in bed, I heard her open a bottle of moisturiser in the bathroom. I thought it was over, but I was wrong. No matter how much my mom expelled her emotions, thoughts of worry and anger wouldn't give her peace. She came back into the room for one final time that night. She cast a look at the walls above our beds and plucked every poster down, one by one.

Pop, pop, pop.

"No!" I screamed. "Not the posters!" For months we hadn't bought ourselves any lunch at school. We'd spent every cent we had on the magazines Ćao[30] and Pop Rock[31] to get those posters. Now, in a matter of seconds, our collection was gone.

My sister leaned against the wall. She held the tattered shreds of a poster, and I looked at her and my mother in disbelief.

"Now it's over!" My mom was theatrical when she asserted her dominance. "I don't want to hear about Electric Company in this house ever again!" That's how she re-christened the band Ekatarina Velika, making me burst into laughter and never forget this moment.

---

30 *Ciao*, Belgrade's music magazine for teenagers. It was published twice a month, from 1988 to 1994. With each purchase, one would get a poster of the most popular pop rock stars of the time.

31 A music magazine that started as *Rock 82* and then became *Pop Rock* magazine in 1988. The last issue was released in December 1990.

CHAPTER FIVE
High School (1991–1995)

One spring, at the beginning of the 1990s, my brother brought home a mixed breed dog he'd found on the street. I don't remember who suggested the name Dora, but I recall no one argued the choice. She was an adorable female puppy that looked somewhat like a corgi and also a pinscher, with two shades of brown and white hair, and was not older than three months, as we would soon learn.

Dora had had a rough start as she spent some weeks on the street and then a few days in our neighbour's condo. When she finally got into my brother's hands, he knew she would find a place in our home.

For years, we had tried to convince our parents to let us have a pet. Every single time, we were told we didn't have enough space.

"We need a yard. Dogs need space to run and play. It's cruel to keep an animal in an apartment." And that was the end of the discussion.

But this situation was different. The dog was no longer something we imagined we'd have. She was already in our apartment.

Both Mom and Dad reacted to the new situation in their own way. Dad provoked us, saying, "You haven't shown you're ready for this kind of responsibility."

"No way, this is not happening. There are already five of us in this household," Mom added. She was certain this was just one more of our whims and another job for her.

"We promise we'll look after her," we countered. We continued repeating our promises over and over until they surrendered. They let us know Dora could stay as long as we would take care of her. If not, she would be sent away.

We took the responsibility seriously and did everything that was expected. After all, there were three of us, and since we had opposite shifts in school, morning and afternoon, we had enough time to devote ourselves to her. Within a few weeks, the tension eased. Dora soon stole our parents' hearts, and we started fighting about who'd get to take her for a walk or in whose bed she'd sleep that night.

She became a key member of the family. Until then, there had been one empty place at our dinner table, and now, for every meal, it was taken. We wrote her name on the list of tenants, as we wanted other people to treat her as an equal member of our household. And they did. In the years to come, every postcard our friends sent included a greeting for her too.

When Dora came into my life, I couldn't imagine how much her presence would impact me. I also didn't know how much it would hurt when she left us. In the fifteen years we spent together, she slowly changed my habits and pushed me in different directions. There were times when she wanted to get out and run and play, while I desired to just close the shutters and give up on the day. But this was how she led me into situations that I'd have otherwise missed, or got me into contact with people I wouldn't normally interact with. With her by my side, I reconnected with my elementary school friends. I was also introduced to some neighbours I never had the opportunity to meet before.

We had all sorts of adventures together. She was my travelling companion on Saturdays when the whole school gathered to play sports. I led her across half the city to parties, to my friends' houses for coffee, and to swim in the Danube River. In the years I studied literature and read in silence for hours, she would always lay on my parents' bed behind my desk and keep me company. When I started University, I moved my desk into their room, the farthest from the entrance, as I was looking for a quiet place where I could learn. Many times, I ended up feeling excluded from the rest of my family and the world itself, which wasn't always bad, though it was so very lonely. I was convinced she felt everything I felt, because when I was distressed she'd come over to me, and with a touch of her paw or a quiet bark, distract me from worrying thoughts.

Today, I actually don't know who really needed who more. I used to believe I had to look after her, but now I know she took care of me as well. She managed to pull me into a different state of being, where I became calmer and felt better about myself and life in general.

In the meantime, I finished primary school and passed the high school entrance exam. I was excited for this change, and I looked forward to the beginning of the new school year.

Since my early teens, I'd been preoccupied with various activities. I played sports, learned languages, did a stint at a radio station, and learned how to develop photos in an improvised photo lab. Usually, I went along with the friends I considered my tribe. Someone would suggest we go to the school's basketball team training, and before I knew it, I'd be practicing in the hall twice a week, preparing for inter-school competitions. One of my close friends decided in the middle of high school to go to extracurricular music classes, and I joined her. I tried to learn the classical guitar. Despite the encouragement I was given, I gave up. I convinced myself it was already too late to take that road.

Music, however, remained an important part of my life. After my first year of high school, my friends and I went to the Guitar Music Festival[32] in the city of Zaječar.[33] I was so excited about that event. It took a whole summer to convince my father to let me go.

"You are too young to go on your own!" he said. He insisted I wasn't old enough to participate in that type of event. I didn't know what he was talking about, and why he didn't understand how important this was to me. All I dreamed about was to see one of my favourite bands, Atomsko sklonište,[34] on stage. I tried another tactic to get my parents' permission when I lined up my friends in front of them.

"This is who I'm going with." They'd known the boys and girls since they were kids. "This is our tent. I borrowed it from a neighbour, and we're taking a backpack full of stuff."

I had prepared a blanket, flashlight, cans, cutlery, soap, etc. One of my friends had an aunt in

---

32 A music festival held since 1966. This is the longest-running festival in Serbia and Southeast Europe. One part of the festival is a competition between indie bands, and another includes performances by established musicians.

33 A small city in eastern Serbia.

34 *Atomic Shelter* is a rock band from the city of Pula, Croatia. The band was formed in 1977 and named after a 1968 theatre play. Through the years, the band line-up has changed many times, with frontman and bass guitarist Bruno Langer being the one remaining founding member.

Zaječar, and I promised I'd use her phone to call them every day. "All I need is money for the train ticket, food, and some change if I happen to need it."

I repeated my request every day and remained persistent for weeks. Dad waved me away with a hand, showing no intention to yield. Mom recruited my older sister to help her make me give up. For a moment, she swayed me with scary stories of what might happen in situations when I was alone and far from home. But I couldn't stop imagining myself in front of the big stage with music playing on and on for three days. I felt as if I was already a part of that event, and my excitement was stronger than any fears I may have had.

In the end, my father saw me off with a short but firm monologue. "You are on your own out there. Be mindful of what you say and who you share it with. You have to know that everything you do will come with consequences." Then he gave me some money, and I was off!

For years, I lied and said the festival was brilliant. I told people it looked like the American Woodstock[35] and that I was happy to take part in it. But the truth was, the bands I longed to see didn't perform that year. I didn't like camping either, especially not having the

---

35 A music festival held August 15–18, 1969, in Bethel, New York State. Rolling Stone magazine listed it as number 19 in the *"50 Moments That Changed the History of Rock and Roll."* The festival attracted an audience of more than 400,000 people. Some of the performers included Jimi Hendrix; Janis Joplin; The Who; Joan Baez; Grateful Dead; Jefferson Airplane; Santana; Crosby, Stills, Nash, and Young; and Joe Cocker.

bathroom to myself in the morning. The weather was also a problem. During the day, it was unbearably hot, but overnight the temperature would drop and I'd be so cold that I couldn't get warm. I also never forgot the suffering we experienced on our way back to Belgrade. We spent several hours waiting to change trains. We also had to put up with the rudest people I'd ever met. I could hardly wait to see my city again and have my life back.

It's more than enough to say that I never went back to this town or festival, nor did I trust other people's stories about their fabulous times there.

I enjoyed my own little world like I was on a carousel ride. With my head and heels high above the earth, I felt sure and secure in my seat. I reached that point of acceleration when, light as a feather, I walked around with a smile plastered on my face. And right then, the carousel began to slow down.

Even today, I can't remember how it all happened. I recall witnessing some situations that made me feel totally different. There were fewer and fewer joyful turns, but I kept expecting them. Why wouldn't I? Everything I ever knew was like a fairground.

The last spontaneous moment of child-like play came unexpectedly. One afternoon, during my first year of high school, I heard about an amateur theatre group. The group was about to start work in one of Belgrade's neighbourhoods, and the assistant director was checking to see if there were students from my school interested in joining in.

I was, as were two of my girlfriends. We picked up the address and went to check it out. The theatre was located on one of Belgrade's hills on the east side of the city, while my neighbourhood was on the west side. It took me more than an hour to get there because I needed to take two or even three buses. Prior to that moment, I would only go to this area for two reasons: to visit a dear family friend with my family, or, during the summer breaks, to spend time with my brother and friends in a nice, open swimming pool at the local recreation centre.

The members of the theatre group were the biggest reason I enrolled. They were a great mix of people of different ages and different walks of life; some were already university students. Our director was a theatre lover who, as I would get to know later, had worked with young people throughout his life. I liked his teaching methods. He knew how to encourage us to relax and give our best, while learning and practising acting. In a sense, we didn't *do* anything. We just played and talked and laughed a lot. The director generously shared his connections to the city's well-known theatres and made it possible for us to attend rehearsals of professional performances. That year, we saw some of the city's best live shows, and it all happened so spontaneously, as if things like this happened every day and to everybody.

A month or two after we started, a small group of theatre students split off and worked for some time on their own play. I was one of them. We got a new young director, who was calm, thoughtful, and open to hearing any suggestions we had. My girlfriends and I were the youngest in the group, while he and the other students were four or five years older. They were like heroes to us, and we looked up to them and treated them with respect.

Our group would meet up a few times a week, mostly after school. Sometimes I'd come home late, but my parents didn't worry much. They knew where I was, plus I had everything under control at school. My grades were high, as usual, so they didn't find any reason to question how I spent my spare time.

Bijeli klaun[36] was the title of the book we transformed into a play. It was the story of a boy who grew up in a circus, where his parents worked as clowns. He lived on the road, travelling from one place to another, and had no real friends. There was a girl from the circus for whom he had feelings. Like

---

36 *The White Clown* is a book by the Croatian writer, Damir Miloš, published in 1988. It is a story about human uniqueness; it talks about our personal sense of identity and struggles to belong. The book is on the mandatory reading list for 7th grade students in Croatian elementary schools.

many other boys, he was ready for various adventures; only in his case, they were all imaginary battles with a dragon. He had one flaw, and he struggled to accept it: he was colour blind. As colour was very important in the world of clowns, he worried a lot. He saw his difference as a disadvantage, and he hid it from others.

The book itself had and still has a special place in my life. I got my first copy while we were working on the play, and because this experience meant so much to me, I treated the book as if it was a treasure.

During the 1990s, I lent it to a close friend. She knew about my unhealthy attachment to it, and still she ended up losing it. She felt guilty and tried, like I did, to find it in numerous city libraries or to buy it in bookshops. But it wasn't possible. The author was from Croatia, and since Croatia separated from Serbia in the civil war, there was no way we could buy the book anymore. It became a part of a world and country that no longer existed. I needed a few years to come to terms with the fact that the book was lost forever. I truly grieved this loss as I did many losses during that time. Somewhere during those years, I accepted the fact that life was nothing but one endless process of losing everything and everybody, so I let it go. But then, at the very beginning of a new and much brighter phase in my life, in the early 2000s, I received a copy of the *Bijeli klaun* as a present from an acquaintance. I was so moved that I read it at once and cried the whole time. I was again witnessing the powerful impact the book had on my life. It pushed me into a new direction and the path that would bring so much love and happiness my way.

We worked on the *Bijeli klaun* play for several months. I didn't get an important role in the show, and that was fine with me. I mostly played some side characters, and in one scene, along with another girl, I was a tree. If I'm not mistaken, I think it was an oak tree. We both wore brown pants and a white t-shirt with ribbons in various colours as we were meant to evoke the autumn season.

I also had other responsibilities: dimming the lights when necessary, playing some music from backstage, and setting the stage for the next act. I later realized I was truly enchanted by the process of creating a performance, while acting wasn't my thing. I'd like to believe that others from the group, those who had more experience, understood this before me, and I appreciate they didn't hold me back. They gave me time and space to find that out myself.

Our little theatre group clung together as if the world would disappear if we didn't see each other the very next day. We became as close as family members. We celebrated New Year's together, visited each other's homes, and met downtown to chitchat. I put the theatre on the top of my priority list and wouldn't miss any class, even if I had a good reason not to come.

Our premiere was the following spring, and it was a hit. We performed to a full house, something I've never forgotten. I memorized the faces from the audience, the smiles and applause when they called us back onto the stage, and the joy that was in the air that night. We were pleased with what we'd achieved and were filled with the desire to do it all again. We'd already made plans to continue performing anywhere people would want to watch us: on streets, in preschools, or other kids' organizations.

Just around that time, the word *war* crept onto a new page of our story. It was as if I'd been on some other planet until then. Suddenly, I was in unfamiliar territory. That day, the day I heard the word *war*, our group met at the theatre at the usual time. When I entered, I encountered a scene I wasn't expecting. A young student, who played one of the lead roles in our play, sat in a chair with his head in his hands. He was from the Croatian coastline and, if I remember correctly, he was studying at Belgrade University. Somebody from the group approached me and said he'd spoken to his parents the night before. They were frightened by what was happening in the country and insisted he pack up his things and come home straight away.

I remember the tears on his face. Other grown-ups were crying too. Through the whole evening, they didn't say much. They just sat next to him, holding their hands on his shoulders. I was quiet as I stood to the side and watched them. I was afraid to ask anything that could be considered inappropriate. For a long time afterwards, I asked myself if that was really how it all happened. Maybe I misinterpreted something. Back then, I was just a big kid, and I didn't understand much of what was going on.

But there's one thing I'm sure of. Soon after that day, nothing was ever the same again. Our happy, playful, and innocent meetings were replaced by noisy and messy street protests. On our way to school, my classmates and I would stop and listen to what people said. I wasn't at all aware of how dangerous the situation was, nor could I even guess where it would take us. I believed this mess would soon pass, and everything would be as it was before.

I'll always remember the scene at Terazije Square. Hundreds of people were on their knees praying and holding lit candles in their hands. This prayer for peace was like an ancient ritual in which people would find time to stop war for a moment and live freely for a few days before the conflict would start again.

Like a Greek marathon runner, I hurried home to tell my family what was happening in downtown Belgrade. I remember bumping into my mother on the stairs of our building. She held our dog in her arms and was visibly distressed.

"Where've you been?" She raised her voice. "Do you know when school finished?" She was right. I was pretty late. "Your lunch is on the stove. But it's cold. You'll have to heat it up."

"What's with you?" I asked. Her face was all red.

She sighed in frustration. "Your father's gone crazy. I'm going outside to take a walk and calm down."

When I entered the apartment, I was greeted by darkness. And that was strange. There were five of us in my family, which meant there was usually a light on in every corner of the apartment. Dad sat in an armchair in front of the TV as images of frightened people running away from gunfire flashed across the screen. He was swearing. It was the first time I'd ever heard him swear. He stood up and walked in circles, from the armchair to the television, then to the terrace, then back again. As he paced, he ran his hand through the little hair he had on his head.

"Don't turn on the light," he yelled at me. I didn't plan to. I sank into my chair, and I could barely breathe as I watched the TV news and my father's behaviour.

"They're going to kill them all, do you get that?" He looked in my direction, but I doubt he was talking to me. I thought about what he had just said and wondered who was going to kill who.

I had seen that expression on his face before, but even then, I wasn't entirely sure what it meant. As a kid, I didn't like drinking milk. I could be persuaded to drink milk from a carton box, but I couldn't stand the milk they sold in plastic bags. That milk had to be cooked before drinking, and as it cooled down, a layer of thick skin formed on top. I found it disgusting. Every time my parents would tell me this was the best and sweetest bit to drink, I thought I would throw up.

"Gross!" I'd turn my head and beg them not to make me drink it. I poured the whole glass down the sink many times. Once Dad caught me. He stormed over to me and looked straight into my eyes.

"Somebody out there is praying for this glass of milk." His face changed, and rage overtook him. "It could save somebody's life, and you're pouring it out like it's worthless." I cried and promised I would never do it again. When Mom came into the kitchen, he turned to explain what had happened, and I took that moment to run into my room. I stayed there until later that evening.

It was only in the 1990s that I finally understood what he'd been talking about. In less than a year, our whole life became focused only on surviving. Misery and deprivation took over our lives and slowly dissolved first our habits, then our opportunities, and finally our expectations. We lived like we were in an arena; the hungry were on one side, the stuffed on the other. Everywhere I went, I came across scenes I found captured in an old Serbian language proverb: the well-fed man doesn't believe the hungry; the hungry man doesn't understand the well-fed.

My father carried this experience deep within himself. He was born just before the Second World War, and he remembered all too well the turmoil and deprivation in post-war times. He lost his father, who was the breadwinner, in the war. His mother barely managed to provide the basic things. He spent some of his school years in poor boarding homes. He told me about bugs on plates and that he went to bed hungry many times. He shared a story about broken nails and toes from playing football barefoot. When he got sick, they fed him fish oil by force. He hated it and was forever disgusted even with the smell of fish. All the traumas he suppressed would arise when he saw food being thrown away. It was an unbearable inner trigger he couldn't control.

He had that same expression on his face on the day I came home from the protests. I didn't yet understand what was about to come, and he was already reliving the horror he went through once. I only understood later that he was reminded of the experience of dread and helplessness, and it became clear to me that in that moment, although he was unaware of it, some child within him was calling for help: "They're going to kill them all, we're going to go hungry!"

That scene burned into my consciousness and shook up my sense of peace. From that moment on, my family life started to change. Because everything in the outer world was still in its place, I supressed similar episodes for some time and continued to live as I had before.

The new reality knocked on our door again in early spring 1992. My paternal relatives were forced to flee from their village. At one point, there were nine of us in a 2-bedroom apartment.

I experienced all these events as a bystander. I still didn't understand that this drama had something to do with me. Many years would pass before I realized that many of the people who took part in it were also not entirely aware of the life changes that had just taken place. They lived in hope that everything could still be as it was before.

I stayed in my bubble and lived a normal high schooler's life. I met new people every day. I looked forward to new school subjects such as Latin Language or History of Art, and I enjoyed learning new, interesting facts.

Many years later I would find out that, at that same moment, many of my fellow citizens were running away to seek refuge in European countries and across the Atlantic Ocean. Some people chose to go because they didn't want to wear the uniform of any army, some had to leave because they became unwanted overnight, and some had already lost their houses and didn't have any place to go.

The catastrophe, meanwhile, revealed its full face to me. In school, through my friends, and in my neighbourhood, I met people who had lived through awful experiences and situations that were completely unthinkable to me.

Their stories didn't resemble one another, but the ending was always the same. Here are a few of the stories I heard from my peers.

After World War II Yugoslavia was made up of 6 republics: Slovenia, Croatia, Bosnia and Hercegovina, Serbia, Montenegro and Macedonia. From 1991, when the first conflict broke out in Slovenia, Yugoslavia's republics/provinces started splitting into independent countries.

"Dad came home one afternoon in a rush and told us to get ready. He said we were going to some shelter to hide until the madness calmed down. I trusted him and put on my worst clothes because I didn't want to get dirty. I realized we were going somewhere much farther away when I saw that he'd taken us to the airport. My mom, my sister, and I stood in a long line of people who waited to get onto the plane. Everyone believed it was our last chance to get out of Sarajevo City. Dad was scared I'd miss the flight, so he helped me cross over the fence and told me to go on. 'We're right behind you, hurry up and don't worry, everything will be alright,' he lied, to convince me to listen to him. Everything happened so quickly. We got separated in that crowd, and it was only when the doors of the plane closed that I realized I was alone. It was the first time I'd been on a plane. I stood next to some people and didn't know where I was going or where my family was. In half an hour or so, we landed in a place that was unfamiliar to me. Everybody went off in their own directions, while I sat on the curb. I got anxious and began walking around the entrance barrier. By accident, I came across a car and recognized my paternal uncle behind the wheel. I saw my mother and sister in the backseat, looking from the window into a crowd. When they saw me, they sobbed. We hugged and cried like we hadn't seen each other for years. Dad stayed behind. I learned we were going to stay with his family in Serbia and that we weren't going home to Bosnia. Maybe never. I asked myself months later what would have happened if I'd stayed sitting on that curb. Who would I call; where would I go? I didn't even know where I was. Nataša, you haven't got a clue how awful it is to be that scared and helpless."

Another story went like this:

"I was on the Croatian coastline with high school friends. People were talking about war. You could feel hostility, but I kept living my life like none of this mattered to me. At that time, my friends were more important to me than my family. We did everything together. Dad begged me to come to my senses and come to granddad's house, to the village above the city. Granddad was dying. I thought my family was lying and that they'd stop me from seeing my friends, so I refused. But I kept looking at the watch on my wrist. It was a present from my granddad. At one point, I got anxious and called them. Granddad had died, and my friends talked me into going. 'You can't not go to your granddad's funeral!' I got on the bus and that was the last time I was at home, and the last time I saw them. In the meantime, people from both sides, Serbian and Croatian, started fighting. The war began, and my parents sent me to my relatives in Belgrade until the situation calmed down."

And this story:

"My whole life I'd been buying bread in the same shop from a woman I considered as family. And then one *morning she told me to tell my mother that from tomorrow onwards she'd have to find a new shop. I was a little brat; I didn't have a clue what that meant. That same day, people in uniform arrested my dad and my brother. I saw my brother after a few days, but never again my father. He was murdered. We buried Dad in Montenegro, in his hometown, where we fled from Croatia."*

And this sad tale:

"When I was watching news from Croatia, I asked myself, 'Who were these upset and miserable people? How and where did they live?' I had never before seen such misery in my country. I used to say there was no way it could happen here in Bosnia and Hercegovina. And a year later, when we were running away, I saw the same misery in our faces. We were now those people from the news."

These young people were my new fellow citizens. It was easy for me to relate to them as I was listening at home to similar stories about the terrible fates of my own relatives. My grandmother became a refugee, and from that point until her death, she lived in Belgrade. I frequently went to the nearby humanitarian aid centres, instead of her, to pick up a package that had come from overseas. A bag of flour, canned foods and pâtés, powdered milk, soap, sanitary pads, and washing powder.

I stood in line with people who waited for their share, feeling humiliated because they had to stretch out their hands like beggars. Angry at anybody who looked down at them, they blamed my fellow citizens for causing this misery. But, like so many of the people from Belgrade, I felt as miserable as them. I saw powerlessness on every face in my extended family and in my neighbourhood.

After leaving the aid package at my apartment, I'd sit on the bus and listen to people from Belgrade who judged refugees for stealing away the order by which we lived here. They said refugees took jobs that were for our children, and that they were destroying the security we counted on. But I knew that many of those refugees would give everything to be able to go back to their homes.

For years, we all lived in a fear-based reality. Like a virus, it spread from many homes onto the streets and transformed my beautiful city, and my life, to its core.

I don't remember exactly which month it was, but I recall I was in my first year of high school when the teachers hung an exit sign above the blackboards. We had to learn how to be prepared if we were ever attacked. The grown-ups probably thought they still had control of their lives, but the truth was they couldn't imagine they would soon lose their sanity in the battle for survival.

Years of panic and helplessness followed, occasionally exchanged for days of hope that everything would be better in a year or so. We got used to street protests, to ever greater disarray, to things running late like buses and paycheques, or to running out of necessities like food. During the second year of isolation, the city was split up into A, B, and C groups. We alternated between times we had electricity and hot water and times we didn't.

Those were also the years when I heard some Serbian proverbs for the first time in my life.

Man is a wolf to another man.

Kindness and stupidity are blood brothers.

If we're brothers, our money purses aren't brotherly.

Life's a mother to some people, a stepmother to others.

I had the impression I'd stepped out into a whirlwind I couldn't hide from. Nothing I'd experienced up to that point had prepared me, let alone equipped me, to face it. I tried hard to understand the numerous new situations in my life, but they didn't make sense to me. I was overcome by confusion and unrest as I saw a dark shadow falling over everything that surrounded me.

As if this wasn't terrible enough, my relationships with my friends had changed. Different circumstances and experiences distanced me from the people I had seen as being a part of me.

I remember a casual conversation when my friend said she was aware there was a war, but if she hadn't known me, she wouldn't have known how it affected people.

I couldn't believe that was possible. My life had come to a standstill. Everything had become too serious and tragic.

Another time, she complained about her mother. Her mom gave her money to buy a winter jacket she needed for the season, but my friend also purchased a poncho by borrowing money from another girlfriend. My friend's mother told her she wouldn't pay for the poncho and insisted my friend return it right away.

On that day, when I entered their apartment, my friend and her mother were arguing in the living room. After we had retired to her room, my friend whined that her mother made a scene in front of that other girl. "It was so embarrassing!" she said furiously. "What's even worse, after the girl left, my mother annoyed me with her dark stories about tough times and life struggles!" my friend added.

I found myself in an awkward position. Although we were peers, I felt as though I was listening to a tantrum from a kid. I won't lie; the words coming out of my friend's mouth had been, until recently, mine. But now, I was miles away from that life. My friend meant a lot to me, so I remained by her side. But it was clear to me she didn't have a clue what was happening around us. Nor within me. I didn't tell her I thought her mother was a powerful woman who, somehow, kept her kids protected from harsh reality. I had already given up on many things I'd considered normal. I didn't see that as a problem because I had people by my side who were showing me what real problems were.

My surroundings divided into parallel worlds. In the first were those who held their heads above the water, remaining outside the orbit of chaos and helplessness. In the second were those whose lives crumbled into little pieces, and in the third were those who had entered another reality overnight. Their previous life was surgically removed and became something that resembled a dream.

One day I was talking to a classmate who arrived at my school as a refugee, and without thinking first I said, "Sometimes I wish I was in your shoes."

"Are you aware of what you just said?" she asked. "You have no clue how hard it is. Everybody in my house is constantly crying." Then she listed details about her scattered family. And while she talked about the abyss, I saw something else before me.

"I know it sounds crazy, and it is," I said. "But what I see is that you're all in the same boat."

I wasn't a refugee; I was in my hometown, yet it felt as if it was a foreign place. I also didn't know anymore who the *"we"* were. My old sense of self was dissolving. I couldn't find myself in a single one of my relationships, either with family members or friends. This feeling plagued me, but I kept quiet about it.

I couldn't find a reason to talk to people. Why would I? Every time I did, I would discover I couldn't get on with anyone. I felt like I was constantly hitting a wall. As a result, I was either extremely sad or extremely angry.

Time passed, and when I finished high school, I enrolled in a literature course at university. In my first year, on the first pages of my Aesthetics textbook, I read a thought that helped me gain some clarity about what I was experiencing: "All human beings are to be born twice in this life. Once in their mother's pain, a second time in their own."[37]

And that was nothing but a truth for me. Through my own pain, I entered another world, I lived another life, and became another version of myself.

---

[37] A quote from Max Dessoir (1867–1947), a German philosopher and psychologist, and associate of Sigmund Freud.

CHAPTER SIX
New Normal

I needed years to put the pieces together and understand how my social life changed so much in such a short period of time.

At the beginning, I slowly stopped going out as I didn't feel safe on a bus or in the streets, especially during late evenings. I then distanced myself from activities I used to love. There weren't that many after the war had started and our old system of life and education had collapsed. New doors remained closed as I couldn't afford them and also because I had a hard time getting along with the new shared values and mindset. I began withdrawing from gatherings and often said to my parents, "In case someone calls, I am not here."

The girl that used to run around and rack up miles in just a week, ended up sitting indoors every single day, sometimes for eight to ten hours. Although I loved reading and learning, I struggled with that new reality and looked for every chance to be outside and move my body. I appreciated then having a dog and being obligated to go for regular walks, and I also used my spare time to exercise. I made up my own routine and practised by myself in my room, which I continued to do for years after, but there were also times when I was a member of local gym clubs.

I don't remember the exact year, it could have been 1997 or 1998, when my sister and I discovered a nice private studio with small groups and a new approach to body work. It was located in Zemun, in the perfect spot, exactly at the halfway point between our apartment and my sister's workplace.

We would usually meet on Tuesday evenings, around 9 pm, at the main street. We chose a place that was close to both of our bus stops and always full of passers-by. We agreed to wait for each other and walk together along the small unlit street which led to the club.

One Tuesday as I got off the bus, I was almost yelling while I rushed down the sidewalk towards my sister.

"Hey, sorry I'm late. You'll never guess what just happened to me!" For a moment I stopped to adjust my backpack which held my aerobics gear.

She frowned and said sarcastically, "Oh, thank God. You've fallen in love."

I was fifteen minutes late. She didn't like waiting for anybody, especially not when the strong, cold *košava*[38] wind was blowing. It was so cold you could barely stand more than five minutes without freezing.

"Oh, cut it out! That's the last thing I need," I swiftly replied.

"Fine," she said. "So tell me, what happened to you?"

I heard her question but thought about what she had just mentioned. Love. I was so far away from it. I'd broken up with a boyfriend with whom I'd gone through extremely difficult life situations. During the war he came to Belgrade as a refugee. He was a high schooler and lived with his relatives. But after he graduated, he was left to struggle on his own. His family lived miles away, in a war zone, and he saw them only a few times a year. I'd been his girlfriend, but also more than that, as he spent most of his time with my family and friends. Unfortunately, he never saw his family reunite again as he lost his loving father at the end of the war. For a long time, we'd stood firmly together, relying emotionally on each other. But then the time came when both of us went our separate ways.

Many times, I felt unbearably weighed down by life circumstances. I found it so hard to keep my head up, let alone relax and enjoy being young. I'd gotten so used to pressure that the idea of being able to take

---

38 A cold, very squally wind found in parts of Eastern Europe and the Balkans. In the winter it can cause temperatures to drop to around -30°C.

a step into something worthwhile and meaningful seemed impossible.

What love actually was, I wasn't sure. Everywhere around me I saw proof that love was overrated. People just hobbled from one so-called love story to another, from one lie to another. I didn't have the time or the patience to act in that play.

I went quiet and increased my pace so I could keep up with my sister. I didn't realize I hadn't answered her question.

"Hello, Earth is calling to Domentijan[39] or Dositej,[40] or whatever writer you're reading right now." She waved her hand in front of my face. "Come on, concentrate now that you're here. Are you here? Well?"

"What do you mean, well?"

"Well, what happened to you? You said I'd never guess…so, I give up." She rolled her eyes and sighed loudly. I could tell she was barely keeping herself from lashing out at me. Not only was I late, but she had to pull words from my mouth.

"The bus ticket inspector just gave me a free ride. And as if that wasn't strange enough, he stuffed three dinars[41] into my hand for the return ticket. I

---

39 A major figure in medieval Serbian literature (1210–1264). He spent his life as a monk at Hilandar, a Serbian Monastery on Mount Athos in Greece, which itself is an important centre of Eastern Orthodox monasticism.

40 Dositej (1739–1811) was a Serbian teacher, writer, philosopher, polyglot and the First Minister of Education in Serbia. An active protagonist of Serbian national and cultural liberation and transformation, he was considered the best-educated Serb of his time. Dositej never stopped inspiring his countrymen to embrace change and growth.

41 Official currency of the Republic of Serbia, first used in the 13th century.

didn't know what to say to him. He left me totally speechless."

"Speechless?" Her tone was sharp now. "I don't get you at all!" She stopped walking, so I did the same. "How can that even be important to you?" She got angrier. "Can't you hear yourself? Listen, don't keep telling those stupid stories of yours when you're with me. You'll embarrass me."

We didn't share another word that night.

For a long time, I had known that she, as well as the other members of my family, didn't understand me at all. When a crisis hits, I learned, people either pull together tighter or they simply drift apart. I wanted to believe we were the ones from the first group, as we still acted like those, especially in a state of high emergency. But the truth is, the 90s made us make different choices, and we led completely different lives.

On the day the bus inspector gave me a free ride, I wasn't just surprised by his gesture. I was shocked. He treated me like a real human being, and he did so without a second thought. Even today, it is heartbreaking for me to accept the fact that by that moment in the late 1990s, I had already learned to expect anything from people but decency.

The reason I didn't have any money for the bus was because I'd forgotten it. I had hurried to finish a chapter in the book I was reading. As usual, I competed with myself, as I would mark in advance the number of pages I needed to read in one day. If I reached the goal, I would go to aerobics without feeling guilty.

I only realized that I'd gotten carried away with my reading when I got on the bus. Not only was I running late, but I'd also forgotten my money. I'd left it on the kitchen counter. Somehow, I'd grabbed my backpack and my jacket, which I'd pulled on and done up as I ran to the bus stop, but I did not take the money. I planned to get off at the next stop and hoped the ticket inspector would not humiliate me. I remembered even saying a quick prayer. I guess my prayers were heard, as I would get to know soon.

My sister didn't use public transport often. She couldn't know what I experienced on the bus every single day. Just one daily ride would be enough to illustrate how, at the end of the 20th century, one European capital had been transformed into a jungle.

Of course, you could see the same scenes on TV, if you happened to watch it. I heard people say that watching TV was the best shortcut to get a degree in human psychology or sociology. Every live show was filled with personal and collective stories of social madness, but some shows went even further. You would swear you were witnessing complete insanity.

I could talk about the bus rides because I spent so much time on public transport during the 90s. At one point, the city officials brought in something they called private buses. One would think this was the solution for the existing disorder in public transit. We would finally see tidy windows, fresh upholstery, separate doors for bus entrances and exits, maybe even air conditioning. Of course, on these private buses, people would know how to behave. They would be quiet and friendlier; they would offer their seat to pregnant women, to toddlers, or to seniors. But that wasn't the case. The only difference was that there were more of these private buses on the roads, and you had to pay three dinars per ride, whereas the public ones were free of charge. This meant the division between the passengers was now even more obvious. On one side were those who could afford this ride and didn't have to wait, and on the other, those who were forced to literally camp at bus stops as public buses were far less frequent.

I strongly disagreed with this new system, not only because I could not always pay the ticket, but because it was a new type of discrimination.

There were, of course, many people who thought differently.

One woman, whose husband ran his own business, decided to tell me her opinion as we waited for the bus. "I'd never allow myself to be without choices." She thought she was entitled to only high standards which were provided by her husband, not by herself. "Everyone can afford to set that amount of money aside for the bus," she said, mocking the ones who were already ashamed of their new life circumstances.

Another woman finally found her own way to place herself above others. "I've been asking myself when someone would come up with the idea of new bus lines. Ah, those savages!" she said, referring to her neighbours. "Who knows how they lived in the backwaters they came from?"

From the 1950s until the 1990s, my country was socialist, and we were led to believe fairy tales of solidarity and the common good. I grew up in an atmosphere of a strong and welcoming community, but after we entered the early phase of capitalism, we started separating in every way we could. So many people were in a hurry to proclaim themselves as special and, of course, better than everyone else. These so-called individuals, with money-imposed egos and a great lack of integrity, made me sick.

Before the 90s, I used to love bus rides, especially when I enrolled in high school. Nobody could understand why I was going to school on the opposite side of the city. Belgrade had sixteen gymnasiums,[42]

---

[42] A type of secondary school that prepares students for university. The word "gymnasium" was first used in ancient Greece to describe a place for both the physical and intellectual education of young men.

and only three of them were farther away than the one I'd chosen. But I really wanted that one. I knew some interesting facts about it. For example, this school always had good indie bands, and some of them became popular. The year I started, my high school created a student TV station, which broadcast programs from the basement for the whole school. It also had a theatre department for people who were preparing to be actors one day. Through my sister, I already knew some of the students, and thanks to them, I got a glance at the school much sooner than when I officially became a student myself.

Although I knew I would have to change two buses every day, I didn't mind. I thought this would be the best way to get to know every corner of my big city. And that's how I would finally be able to talk to my dad like I couldn't before. He always boasted how, when he was a student, he'd crossed Belgrade on foot, from one end to the other. He knew where every institution was, every bus and tram line, the post offices, the public markets. He'd give me a hard time every time I called a street by the wrong name.

"Do you know where that street is?" He'd then take a paper map of the city out of a drawer and tell me to check it myself. "That street is even farther than you think. You've missed it by a kilometre!" I hoped that one day he wouldn't know where some street was, and I'd be the one giving him a lecture.

But just a year after I got into high school, a year into the war, despite my improved knowledge of city neighbourhoods and how to reach them, I couldn't find my way around with public transport. Buses were always late. The drivers would skip stops or drive with the doors half-open. When going around corners, they performed the kind of manoeuvres that, if you weren't fixed in place and hanging on tightly, would send you to the opposite side of the bus.

People were startled. They would get off at the next stop and wonder what just happened. Some old sense of order still flowed through their veins, so they didn't react. It looked as if it was something happening to somebody else. But soon, after many boundaries were crossed without any logic, people became angrier.

The ticket inspectors behaved like sheriffs. "Tickets, tickets!" they hollered while going through the bus. I saw them as characters from a famous TV series, *Otpisani*,[43] which I grew up watching. They moved in packs, but secretly, without any uniforms or markings. They'd come up to you and ask for your ticket, you'd say you didn't have one, and they'd open their jackets to show you their credentials, which were stuck on the inside. You had to stand up and follow them to the exit. But before you'd even get to the exit

---

43 *Otpisani* translates as *Write-Offs*; a famous Serbian and Yugoslavian TV series from the 1970s, created by Dragan Marković. The series shows the lives of freedom fighters in Belgrade during World War II and achieved cult status among its audience.

door, a second inspector would grab you by the arm, not allowing you to move. You would be frightened and isolated because usually other passengers wouldn't even notice what was going on.

I remember one female inspector who put her hands into one girl's bag. I was sitting next to that girl when she tried to find her monthly student pass. She was sure it was somewhere inside the backpack, so she checked every pocket. I could tell from her face that she didn't have a clue what day it was. I assumed she was into her exams and forgot to check the calendar. It was the first of the month, and the time to renew the pass. The girl found it, only to discover her pass had expired. She apologized and offered to buy a single ticket right away. She wasn't allowed. The ticket inspector took her ID card from her open purse, without even asking. It was clear the girl had to leave the bus with her, or she wouldn't get her ID card back. The inspector wanted to charge her because the fine was probably ten times more expensive than the single ticket, and also, as I quickly learned, the inspectors were getting a cut from those fines.

As time passed, passengers took justice into their own hands. The ones who could, pushed back hard.

"No, I don't have a pass." They remained sitting and looked the inspector right in the face. "I don't even have money for food, let alone a ticket!"

They were not lying. Many people lost their jobs during isolation. The unemployment rate was so high that buying a pass was a luxury many couldn't afford.

Some passengers waited calmly for the ticket inspector to ask. After they had been threatened, they would show their real face.

"So, you're going to throw me out? Really?" They would stand up and prepare for a fight. If the inspector wouldn't back down, he or she would be in real trouble.

"Do yourself a favour and disappear. I don't think you want to be the one I would blame for all of my problems. That'd be the damn biggest mistake you ever made!"

I heard from my girlfriend that one man would literally sit on her lap in the bus. Just like that. Can you believe it? Apparently, he couldn't wait for my friend to get off the bus, and he also wanted to be sure he'd get her seat for himself.

Every day for years, there was another scene played out on public transport. One time, the Number 17 bus I took to school turned around at the Genex Tower[44] and continued its way towards Arsenije Čarnojević Boulevard.[45] The bus was jam-packed,

---

44 Officially named Western City Gate, this 36-story skyscraper was designed by Mihajlo Mitrović in 1977. It is formed by two towers connected with a two-story bridge and features a restaurant at the top.

45 A street in Belgrade, which is the section of the highway that runs through the city. Arsenije Čarnojević was Archbishop of Peć and Serbian Patriarch from 1674 to 1706.

and if you happened to look at it from the outside, you could see it had been leaning to one side for a while. It looked dangerous, like the bus was going to fall over at any moment.

Inside, passengers could barely move their bodies. It was a real struggle to reach the exit door, and I remember needing to push forward several stops ahead of mine. If I didn't, I wouldn't be able to leave the bus.

The same scenario would repeat at every station. The bus would stop, the driver would press the button, but the doors wouldn't open. They couldn't. People were leaning on them. The passengers who wanted to get out would then panic. They pushed and shoved, and sometimes shouted or argued with the ones close to the door. They applied any method they could to make their way to the exit and get off the bus.

For the first few moments after they left, I would inhale and stretch myself, because in the next instant, there would be a wave of new passengers pressing on my back and squashing me. "Hey you, in the middle, shuffle a bit!" I heard them say. Everybody fought to get onto the bus. No one knew when or if the next one would come along.

One day, as I tried to survive my crammed ride to school, there were five young guys standing next to me. They grabbed a hold of each other and looked as if they were about to dance a jig in a circle, but instead they jumped up and down, crying with laughter:

"Where're you now, Guinness? Where're you now, Guinness?" They were alluding to the Guinness World Records. This number of people on the bus that day would have surely found its place on the great list of human achievements, if there had been anyone there to count them.

I laughed and laughed on and off for hours afterwards. I never forgot the scene, as their joke brightened my whole day.

There was, however, one scene I can't bring myself to smile about, not even today. I was sixteen years old and on my way home from school. That day was just one in a row of so-called normal days. I had the usual schedule in school; none of the classes were cut short. It wasn't a working Saturday; sometimes on weekends we would make up classes that were missed due to ongoing civil protests or teachers' strikes. On that extremely ordinary day, there were no protests, no power outages, and nobody thought about ripping the tram off its tracks. I didn't have any plans, especially not the kind that would be normal for teenagers: going out and having fun. I only wanted to get home as quickly as possible and detach from the world.

The bus was full, and I was standing between the first and second doors. I always stood close to the driver, since I'd once seen a bus that almost got cut in half. The bad economy and negligence made things, including buses, stay broken for years. I was scared, and from that moment on, I always tried to be in the front half, even though I still considered a spot on the back platform to be the best place. There were always youngsters there sharing interesting stories and good jokes. What can I say, I chose to stay alive, rather than have fun.

The bus was crowded, and people were heckling other passengers. They elbowed the ribs of people who wanted to get off, they kicked the shins of people getting on. One lady constantly stepped on my foot, which wasn't such a big problem. But when she started snorting and waving her hands in front of my head, because she couldn't reach the handhold, I didn't know what to do. I felt extremely dizzy. There was no air. Plus, it was too noisy.

I tried not to think about what was going on around me and told myself we would soon be at the bus stop close to the post office. That stop was at a crossroads, and many people would get off there to switch to another line. After that, I told myself, everything would be better. The bus would be half empty, and I'd be able to put both feet on the ground.

But the bus moved at a crawl. People hung onto the doors, and the driver couldn't close them properly. I felt so weak and claustrophobic that I decided not to stay on the bus. I'd walk home. I thought anything was better than being trapped in this hell.

"Excuse me, are you getting off at the next stop?" I asked that lady, so we could swap places. I'd be at least a little closer to the door.

"What?" She raised her voice. "Are you serious? I've just gotten myself settled and now you want to get off?" She scowled as though I'd asked something inappropriate.

"Yes, at the next stop, if you'd be so kind." And I tried to move but I couldn't.

She dug in right in front of me and clenched her teeth as the words came pouring out of her mouth. I don't remember the entire monologue, but I do recall her saying something to the tune of how we students, or maybe even everybody else but her, were completely nuts. She claimed we didn't understand a thing, and we didn't care about any kind of order. Which, of course, wasn't the truth. Not that long ago, she continued, people knew how to deal with our kind. They would put a pickaxe in our hands and chase us out at dawn to get to work. We were nothing but deadbeats.

And then she said something I still remember word for word:

"Little girl, if you felt any sympathy for these difficult times your country is going through, you'd cut off your hair!"

For a moment, I froze. Then I pushed past her and got off the bus as if I were running out of a burning building. I was shaking and heard my heart pound in my ears. Her face stuck in my mind. The madness in her eyes, the poison from her mouth. It sucked out all the air we shared in that bus.

I wasn't sure what she really wanted to tell me. There were many possible interpretations. Maybe she just got mad and said everything that was on her mind. My presence would be, in that case, completely irrelevant. Several people told me I should have sworn at her.

"That crazy woman was taking it out on you because you're weak. Start using your power! Next time push back in the same manner," they advised me.

That was how people lived when they were in survival mode. Everybody was walking around with bats in their hands and fighting like savages. There wasn't anything you could do but join them. When everybody around you is growling and biting, is there really any other option than to show your teeth as well?

Words, poisonous and cruel, tense, full of anger and bitterness, became our new way of communicating. If you stopped by the elevator for longer than a minute, you would hear yelling coming from every apartment. This was how people spoke to their neighbours, on the street, in the shops, at the post office, in the bank, or at work. This way of communicating even made its way onto the TV. Everybody hurried to be the first to take a shot at someone.

For a while, we entertained ourselves as we watched the coverage of Parliament. Dear God, what they were doing in there! One threw water on another, others made threats or fought. But they also said many words without any responsibility. The worst part was that, after a while, most people weren't even aware of it. They went as far as to swear that you'd made it all up!

These new ways of relating survived the war time and remained in place long after. One time I went to the post office to pay a bill, and when I got confused about a reference number, the woman behind the counter said: "Maybe you'll learn that by the time you finish university!" Ouch.

Another time, I saw an acquaintance who was pregnant with her second child. I honestly didn't know she was expecting, and I smiled when I saw her. "Wow, you're pregnant again, congratulations!" I said, and she snapped back at me. "What am I supposed to do? Wait until you decide to become a mom? Well, I won't!" Ouch. She probably felt I was judging her.

When I went to get my new driver's licence, I was among the first people who had to go through completely new procedures. I remember I used the winter break to take care of it. Everything was as I expected. I waited for hours to apply, then I was asked to come back another day to bring additional papers as there was an error in the register at the police station. I applied and waited for a few weeks. Then I received a note to come immediately to the police station. It turned out that they had a licence with my name, my information, and my picture, but the signature beneath it belonged to, if I remember correctly, some guy called Dimitrije Pantić. And they made it look like it was all my fault. They didn't apologize; they didn't offer to correct the mistake. The man behind the counter was very clear: "Miss, if you don't need a driver's license, you don't have to do anything. Otherwise, you'll have to repeat the procedure. The counter's right there." Ouch.

The first thing I noticed when I travelled abroad on vacation or to visit friends, was the way people communicated. They didn't hiss. Foreigners were kinder and more accommodating than the people at home, especially the public servants. I noticed the same with TV hosts and their guests.

It was so easy for me to adjust to these pleasant realities in other countries, but every time I went back home, I needed a few weeks to get my bearings.

I remember one particular encounter at the post office in downtown Belgrade. I was busy getting back to the tasks I started before a trip abroad, so I didn't get a chance to see my girlfriend for a week or two. I finally found time to meet her downtown when she mentioned we should go to the local post office first. She had to send a package.

The lady behind the counter was very helpful, and I thanked her a few times and smiled.

My friend touched me on the arm and whispered in my ear: "Listen, I can tell you're on cloud nine, which is great. Don't get me wrong, I love to see you shining. But don't you see the way she's looking at us? And everybody else in this office?" My friend looked serious. "Come on, don't be too friendly. They'll start thinking you're making fun of them, and they'll attack us!" I knew exactly what she was talking about, so I looked down and pulled back.

That was the reality I had lived in since 1992. No wonder it was such an emotional experience for me when the conductor on the bus treated me like I was a human being. My sister didn't see anything special in it, but getting a free ride and money for a return ticket was like reaching another planet to me.

I saw the ticket inspector coming towards me. I was already at the exit door, ready to get off at the next station.

"I'm sorry," I said when he approached me, "I forgot my money." I stood, expecting he would spit out a bunch of insults.

But instead, he said something I wasn't prepared to hear: "It is okay. I understand, just take a seat." He was so calm that I got confused. Maybe this was some new tactic, maybe he wanted me to feel relaxed and let down my guard. "No way," I thought. I'd be an easy target when he suddenly attacked me.

But his body language wasn't telling me he would. I returned to my seat and was on alert, watching him out of the corner of my eye.

In some ways, I was glad I stayed on the bus. It was cold and windy outside. The bus was half empty. Nobody sane would go out in that kind of weather unless they really needed to.

The inspector didn't go away. He stayed at the door as he continued talking in his kind manner.

"Where are you off to?"

I was being polite when I answered.

"I'm clearing my head and meeting my sister for an aerobics class," I said. "I've been studying all day." I tried to sound relaxed so he wouldn't sense my fear.

"I knew you would say that," he replied with a smile. "You remind me of my daughter. The only break she takes during the day is a brisk walk in our neighbourhood."

Then, as though he hadn't noticed that I was keeping my distance, he sat down next to me and added, "She goes into her room to study after breakfast and doesn't come out again until late evening. Maybe just for lunch. And it's like that every single day. I am so angry hearing people saying that a university diploma's just a piece of paper. Nobody today respects the hard work and effort. I feel sorry for your generation. You didn't pick a good time to be young."

I stared straight ahead and kept quiet. Suddenly, I felt an inner shake-up, as if my hormones were raging. I became overwhelmed with emotions.

This man's kindness had moved me. I was in a constant struggle to learn how to be tougher, how not to care, but now one kind word had gotten under my skin, and I almost cried. I remembered every detail of that encounter as a part of me wanted to believe that, beneath the layers of ever-present rudeness in my society, people like him still existed.

I looked at him and smiled.

The bus stopped. It was a new bus station, and he stood up to check other passengers.

"Just keep sitting," he said and took a few steps forward. Then he stopped and turned. From the expression on his face, I guessed that he wanted to add something.

"Yes, Sir?" I prompted.

"It's nighttime. I am wondering how you are going to get back home." He was concerned and, at first, I didn't know where this was leading.

"My sister's waiting for me." In a second, I realized why he was asking. "Everything is fine. I will be okay."

He slipped three dinars into my palm, closed my fist and said, "If she comes, you are good, but if she doesn't, here's the money for the ticket. Take care, kiddo!" and he left.

CHAPTER SEVEN
Years of Isolation: Stress and Harm

The years passed. I was now in my early twenties, but it didn't feel that way. It was as if time had stood still, and I just repeated the same day, over and over.

For a long, long time, I didn't leave the city or go on a decent vacation. Even if I had some breaks, everything was so short-lived that it didn't bring the much-needed peace and rest I craved. I would mostly hang out in my friends' apartments and always with the same small group of people: girls from the neighbourhood, some from high school, and the ones I studied with.

At that time, I was considered an adult though I still lived with my parents – a situation that continues to this day for many youth and young adults in Serbia. In some ways, that was a good thing as I didn't have to struggle to survive. Times were tough even for people who hadn't lost their jobs. No paycheques on time, no regular work hours, no workers' rights. Most employees were putting up with any conditions just to make ends meet. I concluded it wasn't worth it for me to give up university and enter the workforce just to be humiliated and abused.

I focused on my studies instead and found meaning and hope in the corridors of my school department, in lecture halls, and in city libraries. I dove into my books with ease, investing my whole self into preparation for classes and exams. Those daily tasks and the face-to-face contact with other students and professors gave me direction and a safe haven.

However, as I dove deeper into literature, I shifted my perspective on life. It was more than discouraging to open my eyes to the fact that people had tortured each other since the beginning of the world. I became aware that trauma, suffering, and fear were part of the human condition. And we were blindly repeating those vicious cycles from generation to generation.

I doubted the future would bring anything better, and that made me anxious and irritable. I got sick often and easily. An ordinary cold would last for weeks. I visibly lost weight and had to get a lot of bloodwork done. For months and years, I relied on all kinds of medications and supplements.

I tried to find a solution to my state of being. I visited the doctor's office regularly, I read magazines about healthy eating, and listened to people who were trying out alternative medicines. I wanted to help myself, but it wasn't easy. Mr. Chaos, as I dubbed my unrest, turned into a tyrant and set the new course of my life. He knew how to drive me around, without any order or goal, until I became disoriented.

One day, as my sister was preparing to go out, she said, "Dad says you've found a new cosmetologist."

"Yeah, your good friend recommended her."

My sister trusted her friend. They'd known each other since primary school. Both she and I had problems with our skin, so every day my sister had to listen to either one of us complaining about it.

"What's the cosmetologist like?" my sister asked.

"This one is a real character," I replied and added, "She has a radical approach."

"What does she do?" We were chatting while my sister was looking through her wardrobe, deciding which dress to wear on her night out.

"She has this special technique," I explained. "She uses chicken meat, mostly chicken breasts. She dips them in some kind of antibiotics, then she stretches them out across the skin until it absorbs them." I babbled on, describing the process in detail.

I wasn't questioning the new facial. Desperate to find a solution for quite some time, I was testing pretty much every option I heard about. There were the famous local Doroslovac face lotion,[46] milk of sulphur, special soaps, plant-based steams and poultices, classic treatments with needles, and even antibiotics.

I looked over to my sister and noticed she'd stopped getting ready. She stood there, dress over her head, hands up in the air, while the fabric gathered around her neck. It was as if my words had startled her so much that she'd forgotten how to pull the dress down.

"She does what?" I could see her face. Her eyes bulged. "You're joking, right?" She scanned me from head to toe and then added, "I can tell you're not joking. Jesus Christ, you've lost your mind!"

"What are you saying?" Her response surprised me.

"Hold on, I still don't get something," she continued. "Dad's buying you chicken and he knows what it's for?"

"Yes," I said.

Then she went nuts.

"You are all completely crazy! All three of you! The only thing I don't know is which one of you is the biggest fool: that woman, you, or Dad. I can't believe this!" She repeated this several times as she shook her head in disbelief.

---

46 A face lotion for oily and acne prone skin based on salicylic acid. It was the most recommended lotion that could be easily purchased in the pharmacy without prescription. Doroslovac lotion is still widely used in Serbia.

Still talking, she entered the living room and faced our dad. Every single word she said added fuel to the fire, but she wouldn't give up. Dad defended himself and said he wanted to help me. He didn't even ask what it was for. Mom finally learned about it. The drama was complete.

"You will take me to her tomorrow," my sister demanded. "I want to meet her. I want her to help me." She emphasized every personal pronoun in a tone of voice that rang through the room. "She's a fraud. It's so obvious. You'd have to be blind not to see it." She was shaming me. "What were you thinking? You're bringing her a free lunch. I wish I could see what's going on inside your head!"

She stormed out of the room. A few moments later, I heard her dialling the telephone to check with her friend whether all this was true.

The very next day, she went with me to see the cosmetologist. She listened, supposedly with interest, to what the woman had to say and then rudely asked whether she could have the treatment without the chicken breasts. The cosmetologist clearly saw what kind of customer my sister was and hurried to see us out. Later that evening, the cosmetologist sent a message via my sister's friend that it would be better if I found someone else to help me.

I remember that episode clearly and still think about it from time to time. Sometimes I can't believe the girl in that story is me, but then again, other times I can. I was desperate for a solution. I had tried everything and got to the edge of hope, willing to believe in the craziest things.

When I now look back, I know that restless younger me was wandering around helplessly. That's why I don't judge her, and I am not at all ashamed of her.

Before the 1990s, I had never heard about quack doctors. Suddenly, you could find them all over the city. They grew like mushrooms, almost overnight. I heard about them through word of mouth. People I knew would mention their problems, and because I could relate to them, I would ask for the contact. The person on the other end knew how miserable and hopeless people were, and they used the situations to guarantee what we craved the most: relief. We would buy into their every promise, without even asking the price.

After some time listening to many similar stories from my friends and acquaintances, I realized I was just one in a mass of people who'd been cheated. Back then, we couldn't do much about it. I don't ever recall hearing someone filing a report to an official or institution. Instead, left to deal with those bluffers on their own, people turned their experiences into jokes.

I'd never have resorted to quacks if I'd been able to find a single helpful person in any of Belgrade's health centres and clinics. Up until the 1990s, I'd never needed them. During my childhood, I hadn't ever heard my parents talk about illness. We didn't have an arsenal of pills, nor did we feel the need to reach for them. We were all very resilient and healthy.

I clearly remember only two medicines that left a mark on my entire childhood. I thought of them as magical cures which jumped straight out from Sport Billy's[47] bag. When a rest, lots of laughter, warm tea, or soup couldn't get rid of my fatigue and sore throat, my parents would give me Aspirin. It was placed in a little green box, similar to the one that bubble-gum cigarettes came in. I was allowed to take one, and that was it. The pain disappeared overnight. The second medicine was powdered bacitracin in a small orange bottle. It's like today's Neosporin. When we'd come home from the playground scratched up, Dad would treat us one by one by dabbing a small dose on our wounds. He would then tell us not to worry, because the wound would heal soon. I immediately stopped crying and felt calmer. I believed him when he assured me the bones underneath the scraped elbows or knees would now be even stronger.

---

47 A 1980 European television cartoon. Sport Billy is a boy from the planet Olympus, which is populated with athletic beings. He travels to Earth with two companions, a girl named Lilly and Willy the dog, promoting teamwork. Through 26 episodes, he battles the evil Queen Vanda, whose mission is to destroy sports and break the spirit of fairness. Sport Billy was adopted by FIFA as a Fair Play Mascot for subsequent FIFA World Cups.

YEARS OF ISOLATION: STRESS AND HARM

I was never absent from school. In the 1980s, we used to have organized mandatory medical check-ups at the end of every school year. Because I was a good student, with my teacher's permission the doctors on duty would give me seven free days as a prize. I never used them as I didn't want to miss a school day.

But that was back when I was an elementary school student. Now, I had so many health problems that I felt overwhelmed and lost. I constantly asked myself what I was doing wrong. I ate the same things as the rest of my family. I breathed the same air. But somehow, I was the only one continually going to check-ups, yet feeling exhausted night and day.

The doctors weren't helpful at all.

"You need to eat horsemeat," one doctor told me. I shrugged. Horsemeat? Really? In Serbia in the 90s you would be happy to eat any protein on a daily basis. Most of us couldn't afford to eat chicken, let alone horsemeat.

"That girl is on a diet; she wants to be fit and doesn't care about her well-being." I heard their snide comments behind me while I was leaving the health unit. They actually didn't even care if I could hear them.

I remember the first time I had an allergic reaction. I was seventeen and on my way to school. I was sitting on a bus and suddenly felt dizzy. I couldn't breathe, and my eyesight became blurred. Parts of my face started to sting, and I didn't know what was happening to me. I panicked. Luckily, my boyfriend was next to me and helped me get off the bus. The local health centre was close by, and he supported me all the way to the entrance. By the time I walked in, my eyelids, lips, and cheeks were puffy. My face had grown into one shapeless mass. People ran away from me in the hall and in the waiting room. Others turned their heads away. I felt like I was in a scene from a local film about smallpox victims, *Variola Vera*.[48]

Within moments, the doctors had me on a bed and pumped adrenaline into me. I had been lying in the clinic for some time when they explained I should go straight to the hospital. I had to do it on my own because the health centre only had limited supplies of injections, and they didn't have enough fuel for their ambulance. Besides, it was only available for life-threatening situations.

Thank God I could rely on my boyfriend to be there with me. An hour after entering the clinic, we headed for the bus. We ran into my mother, who was on her way home from work. She didn't expect to see me, especially not in that condition. She burst into

---

48 A 1982 film about the 1972 Yugoslav smallpox outbreak and the events related to the epidemic. Goran Marković won first prize for best director and best screenplay at the 1982 Valencia Film Festival.

tears the moment she saw me. She assumed I'd been in a car accident. My face was still very swollen.

All three of us went to the hospital together, and I remained there until later that evening. They gave me lots of drugs and did blood examinations, but they couldn't trace the root of such a strong bodily reaction. They advised me to continue with the allergy pills and rest for the next few days.

The same story continued for years: unclear diagnoses and inadequate treatments. Doctors increased my dosage of antibiotics from one week to the next, as though they were sweets, and sent me from one specialist to another. They fumbled around in the dark until one word became ubiquitous in our daily lives: stress.

While it was good to know what might be causing my ailments, I didn't know how to deal with stress. I wasn't sure what to do. I was told the best thing for me would be to spend ten days in the mountains during winter, and then ten days on the coastline during summer. I couldn't help but wonder what world those people were living in. For hundreds of thousands of people, a vacation had become an unattainable luxury long ago. And also, what was I going to do with the rest of the three hundred and forty-five days of the year, when all the paths towards some kind of peaceful existence had become impassable?

I wasn't alone in this struggle. We were living in the shadow of recent war and a society that was in transition. Our lives were filled with survival struggles and constant worry. Illness entered almost every home, and by the end of the 1990s, I didn't know many families that had remained untouched by it. Along with the uncertainty of our diagnoses, we had to face the inappropriate behaviour of medical staff. They became mercenaries, little gods who made careless remarks and behaved irresponsibly, without any consequences.

For years, I tried to control my anger and look at them without resentment. I would list all the excuses in my head: they worked in impossible conditions, were overburdened, didn't have the funding, and also had children or parents they were taking care of. But it didn't help much, as I never regained my trust in them.

I was left to look for solutions elsewhere, and I tried different medical traditions. Along the way, I gathered various pieces of information which helped me learn how to calm myself and take care of my well-being. With years passing by, I continued to educate myself and finally discovered new ways of being. But I still haven't healed from that old wound as I never forgot how the medical staff treated me and those dear to me.

One autumn, after lunch, Mom called my sister, my brother, and me to the table.

"We need to talk," she said.

"What's happened?" We looked at each other.

"Dad's having prostate surgery next week. You need to help me." She listed obligations such as taking care of the house, talking with Dad, answering the telephone, arranging transport, looking after the dog, and so on.

I was surprised.

My father was an "old school" type of man. Simple, with both feet on the ground, and strong self-discipline. As far as I could remember, he followed specific daily routines: he ate on time, took regular naps, went for walks, and was always in bed at the same time. He was ten years older than my mom, but no one would have guessed that. He was always fairly agile, and until then he'd never had any problems health-wise. In all my twenty-something years, I'd never seen him sick in bed. Here and there he'd catch a cold, but after a day or two, he was up again, ready to engage and contribute.

This time it was different. He was quiet and kept to his room. His eyes were often glassy and his movements full of fear. Although he was never hospitalized, my dad didn't like health centres, needles, or the sense of helplessness that comes with disease. We knew that nobody should say anything that might dishearten him.

We visited him the day after he was admitted. He showed us his room and introduced us to the people he'd befriended. We all shook hands and greeted them with compassion. After fifteen minutes, we went out into the hallway to talk to Dad's doctor. We didn't expect to find out that Dad might not be able to have the operation any time soon. Because of the isolation and tremendous deficits in supplies, the hospitals needed us to provide them with essential medical equipment: a compress cloth, band aids, thread, gauze, disinfectants, etc. The doctor said Dad could be operated on as early as tomorrow morning, as long as we had the items on the list. Nothing was a big problem, he concluded, except the catheter. For months they'd been sending people home because they couldn't find a catheter anywhere in Belgrade.

"That's something outside of my control," the doctor added, reminding us to contact him if or when we bought it. Then he left.

Dad stood still. Mom was anxious, and she went to find a place to have a cigarette. "Don't worry," I said, trying to cheer him up. "We'll figure it out." He looked discouraged, then turned and went back to his room.

My sister, my brother, and I scattered throughout the area. The hospital was in our part of the city, and we knew the neighbourhood very well. There were some hidden pharmacies most people didn't know about, and we believed one might have a catheter in store.

We walked into the closest one, right across the street from the hospital. It was the biggest, and I assumed we would find most of the things from our list there. The young woman behind the counter checked off each item on the paper, confirming that nothing was a problem except the catheter. "There's a tremendous demand for them," she explained.

A middle-aged man appeared from behind one door, and I knew, just by looking at the woman's body language, that he was the owner.

"I've ordered them," he said. "You won't find them anywhere. I've already tried."

We shared few words while I was putting the items in a bag. Most of them were there, which was enough to make me hopeful. After I paid, I thanked them with a smile and left.

My siblings and I decided my sister would take one side of the street, and my brother and I would take the other. We kept going and entered every pharmacy, just to hear the same story: no catheter.

Every time I would leave a store, I'd look across the street to see my sister's face and check if she'd had any luck. I would find her shaking her head. After a while, I became frustrated, but still expected everything would turn out all right.

And then, as if something had guided us to one small street, I came across a house with a little pharmacy in the basement. I swore I hadn't seen it before, and I rushed in with my brother.

I held my breath as I asked the woman over the counter about the catheter.

"I have it." She said it just like that, as if I'd asked for a band aid.

For a few seconds, I was pretty conflicted. I felt both excitement and disbelief. But then, I almost screamed.

"I knew it! I had a crazy feeling we'd find it." I turned to my brother and could see him smiling, too.

The woman listened to my story about Dad's illness and the list we were given. She didn't know anything about the shortage in the hospital, she told me, when she handed me the catheter with my receipt. "Please, tell the people who need it that I've got more." I thanked her and promised I would.

We hurried out to find our sister and share the news. She saw us leaving the pharmacy, and before we even approached her, she could tell we had succeeded.

"We've made it!" I cheered.

On our way back to the hospital, we decided to go back to the first pharmacy as I realized we were still missing one or two little items. The pharmacy owner was behind the counter when we entered the store. He was surprised to see us again. With the broadest smile in the world I said, "You're not going to believe this!"

As I waited for him to get the last few items, I told him about our find. I was in my own world, and I didn't expect what came next.

"Huh, that useless woman has catheters?" His words expressed an arrogant contempt for the other pharmacist. I flinched. "If I'd known, I'd have bought them up this morning. I could've sold them to you now for double the price."

He said that right to my face, without shame.

I was speechless and stared at him with my mouth half-open.

Everything that happened in the pharmacy from that moment on was somewhat of a blur. Someone from behind me placed a hand on my shoulder and tried to move me aside. I turned to see my brother with a clenched fist. He stepped forward to hit the pharmacist, but punched the counter instead. All the products lined up on it tumbled and fell to the floor.

"That's for my dad, you idiot!" my brother hollered behind me. It was then I realized what was behind his calm face and silence. All the tension he was holding inside flowed out in a mass of profanities that tore through the pharmacy.

"Stop!" I said, as he brandished his fists above my head.

"Stop it!" I heard my sister. "Leave him. Don't you see he's a bastard?" She tried to push my brother back.

My brother was furious and continued to scream as he watched the pharmacist over the counter pick up the phone.

"You're calling the cops! Good choice!" My brother was straining against us. "Call them! Better them picking me up than an ambulance coming to pick you up," he yelled through a clenched jaw. "I'm going to kill you!"

A few moments later, my sister and I climbed the stairs to the ward where Dad was staying. We left our brother on the street, explaining the situation to a police officer. They had arrived in under five minutes, as the police station was just two blocks away. As we got to know later, it wasn't the first time they'd been called to intervene in that same store. The owner was well-known for his rude behaviour. The officers filed a report, yet there were no charges. My brother was free to go.

Mom had just left Dad's room and was in the hallway when we walked up.

"You found it?" she sighed. We nodded. A smile slowly spread across her face.

"It's all here," I showed her the bag. "Now we have to find the doctor." My sister and I headed to his office.

"Just a second!" For some reason Mom stopped us.

She calmly examined my sister and me.

"Look at you!" She touched my face. "Were you at a boxing match or the pharmacy?"

I was silent because I didn't know if I wanted to say anything. My sister approached, fixed my hair, and wiped mascara from my eyelid and from under my eyes. I hadn't realized what a mess I was.

"The washroom is over there." Mom pointed to the door on the right. "Clean yourself up and then go to the doctor's office."

My sister and I took a step towards the washroom as Mom asked where our brother was. "He's waiting outside," my sister replied, but I don't know if Mom heard. She was already going into Dad's room to share the good news.

The two of us exchanged a look, knowing that we would never tell her the whole story.

CHAPTER EIGHT
Toxicity and Disconnection

People love to say and write that adversity brings people together. Those are the moments, they claim, when our superficial differences can be easily erased and left behind. Once we undergo the same struggles, our common needs awaken us to the importance of sharing.

Although I honestly wanted to believe in this, my life experience was quite different. I went through some really harsh times and faced many adversities, but I don't recall experiencing compassion and togetherness. The fact is, it was right then I became aware of how divided the world really was.

Instead of unity, everywhere I looked I saw a line of representatives from numerous warring camps. On one side there were those who were born here, on the other those who had come from elsewhere; then the individuals from the prominent upper crust were

TOXICITY AND DISCONNECTION

pitted against those without prospects of a bright future. I learned there were also the so-called socially intelligent people and a vast group labelled as losers. The former would sometimes be referred to as the ones who knew what they wanted and did what it took to get it, and the latter were considered simply full of hot air.

I somehow belonged to both sides, yet I felt as if I didn't belong anywhere. That's how I found out that you can spend a decade living in a full house, in a city of two million people, and feel utterly alone.

Divisions between people brought forward the emotion of shame. To avoid its discomfort, we started making jokes about pretty much everything. For example, in those long years of isolation, we made cakes that were known as embargo cakes. Instead of eggs, butter, vanilla extract, chocolate and so on, these cakes were made out of nothing but flour and homemade jam. Heaven knows, you can't destroy us! All that Serbs need are certain conditions, and they'll use their inventive minds to come up with the impossible. There you go world, a Sunday dessert without eggs!

We came up with a list of excuses for why we lived or behaved a certain way, so we could feel slightly better about ourselves. We said we would fix our apartments or houses if only the construction workers had been more skillful. Somehow, we couldn't trust them anymore. The same went for tailors; it's not that we didn't need a new coat, but it was they who weren't professional enough and only wanted to rip us off.

People would project their insecurities and inadequacies onto others and come across as real assholes, or they would put their heads down and try to preserve their dignity. It wasn't safe or smart to open up and share your vulnerabilities, so we learned to hide them. We didn't mention where we bought our underwear, that we couldn't afford proper sanitary pads, or didn't have money and a decent wardrobe for a night out. I remember sitting in the library, day after day for hours, reading and studying from the books I couldn't take out of the building. But theoretically I could have photocopied the pages. I thought up hundreds of reasons as to why I didn't want to photocopy them, but never mentioned the main reason: money.

Like everyone else, I thought my struggles were the hardest and couldn't see a way out. I could have dealt with misfortune easily if only I was living in a society where a clean suit, and a sense of responsibility and integrity, were the shared values. But that wasn't the case. Times had changed, and suddenly everybody who had any power mocked the ones who didn't. They'd say anything to destroy a person's self-worth and make them feel as tiny as a grain of sand.

People who had lost their houses and careers overnight couldn't re-orient themselves and get back on their feet. I heard them say, "Nothing makes sense. We can't go on living like this."

And yet, life moved forward, in a direction that seemed to be less and less understandable. Anything they knew until then and considered to be normal, didn't work anymore. They didn't know what to accept. They wondered if, without a roof over their heads, they'd become just numbers. They felt like a statistic and that they no longer existed as human beings.

I remember an episode with my uncle. As a child, I didn't realize how influential he was and how much he was attached to his surroundings. Months into the war, he was stubborn and refused to leave his land. He didn't want to choose sides and wear a uniform, but in the second year, after his son ended up in prison, he was forced to do so. All he dreamed about was the day the war would be over and he would go back home to the life he'd had before.

I visited him one summer after the war, when I was already in my twenties. Those were the years he and my aunt temporarily lived in a refugee camp on the opposite side of Bosnia and Hercegovina, their homeland. He was glad I'd come, and he led me around the centre to introduce me to his new neighbours. I also got to see my first and second cousins, people I either hadn't ever met or hadn't seen since I was in middle school. We had all changed a lot.

The first night in the camp, I was preparing to go out and catch up with my relatives. My uncle called me over. He opened his wallet and took out the largest banknote from it. He asked me to promise I would have fun and spend it all.

At first, I didn't want to take the money. I already had enough of my own, and I also felt ashamed to take from someone in his position. But he wouldn't take no for an answer, so I surrendered.

"I know you've got money, but that's not the point," he said. "If you don't want to enjoy yourself, then do it for me." He then turned his back and looked out the window.

I tried to persuade my aunt to take the money back, but she said no too. As I was putting my shoes on, ready to leave the room, I heard him talking to himself.

"It's so good you came. It's so good to know that somebody still remembers me."

Even today, even when I don't want to, I can sense shame in people around me. I am so familiar with this intense feeling of discomfort that I understand why people want so badly to run away and hide. We all seek understanding and acceptance, but somehow we all think it will come from the outside, that other people will free us. I have lived enough that I know this has never been the case. Blessed are the ones who first reach within.

Years before, in the middle of the 1990s, I was thrilled to enrol in my second year of university earlier than I thought I would. In the first round of June exams, I'd met the requirements by passing my tests with great grades. I was so happy I could devote myself to my remaining exams with ease, and spend the summer without worry. It seemed to me, and it's often the case, that when something good happened, other even better things would quickly follow.

I wanted to mark the occasion, so one day I visited my sister at her workplace in the mall. We planned to relax and have a coffee during her lunch break, but the day was too busy. We spent some time together, and I ended up browsing around while she got back to her customers. Right across from her store in the mall, I ran into two girls, about six or seven years old. They were the children of my sister's acquaintances, the women who worked in shops nearby.

The girls had just met, they told me, and they were playing with some dolls as if they'd been doing that together forever. In a world with no barriers, they imagined castles and balls, listened to one another in bursts, and built their own fantastical world.

I enjoyed watching them and thinking how there were certain spaces where the monsters of division couldn't burrow into, even if they wanted to. "They can't destroy childhood," I exulted. "Kids are out of their reach."

Out of nowhere, in the middle of the game, one of the girls lifted an eyebrow the way that grown-ups do, and asked the other girl, "Where does your mom work?"

Without thinking, she gestured and said, "There, in that shop."

"Hmm," the first girl said. "Does she own the business, or does she just work there?"

I know children mimic adults, and I'm aware they don't understand a lot of the things they say, but the scene that unfolded before me was quite disturbing. I noticed the girl whose mother worked in the shop had gone quiet. She probably realized from the tone and expression of the other girl that something wasn't right. She didn't say anything. She simply straightened up and stood a foot away from her companion. She held the hem of her dress in one hand, and in the other, a doll. I watched her withdraw as if she had found a wall where she could hide herself away.

Just like that, the game they'd been playing was over.

I was wrong. Nothing can put the monster on a leash. He won. He found the way to slither into children's games and shame them, too.

I was overcome with fury. At first, I wanted to face the mother of the arrogant girl, but I knew that if I said anything, I'd end up making a scene. Back then, I couldn't hold myself together and confront the person in a kind manner. So instead, I hurried to say goodbye to my sister and left.

I asked myself how it was possible that I kept coming across these scenes. Everywhere I looked, I saw masses of scared and helpless people hiding from their own shadows. They kept looking for an escape, but couldn't find a safe haven anywhere, not even in a kind word of another human. I couldn't accept this fact. Maybe it was all just me; maybe I didn't get it right?

I cried when I left the mall. That scene showed me something I'd read for my literature exam. It was by a critic who'd once disparaged a text written by the realist writer Ivo Ćipiko.[49] Ivo wrote a lot about the adversity he witnessed in his local community, and the critic approved of Ćipiko's style but gave harsh feedback about his depressed world views.

"Dear Author, I think you already made a good illustration of the human condition by writing about people who lived in such poverty that they had to rely on the moneylenders to survive. Yes, we got the picture, and we understood the reason they lost their

---

49 A Serbian writer originally from Dalmatia, Croatia (1869–1923). In his novels, Ivo presented the life struggles of the so-called simple world of the south Adriatic coastline.

hopes and decided to leave their country. But I think you went too far when you sent the people left behind into another turmoil. On top of all their struggles, they now had to deal with a drought. That's unheard of! Literary endeavours, as you know, must be, as in life, properly motivated, or readers won't be able to relate. Why did you, for God's sake, create so much sorrow? Enough is enough."

Just when I'd begun to think the same while looking at the world around me, I'd see a staircase that led ever deeper down, seemingly without any good reason. It was as though somebody had pulled clouds over the joy I'd felt that very morning. I couldn't feel it anymore. All I could do was write this sorrowful epilogue to yet another day:

> *For every moment of joy that warms me and*
> *lifts me up,*
> *I see a gravestone spring up, or someone*
> *hangs up a death notice.*
> *As a rule, I always see my name*
> *in the obituary,*
> *On the space left for the ones*
> *who are mourning.*

I told that story to a friend on the bus the next day. I knew I could share my feelings with him. We'd been friends since we were kids. We went to the same kindergarten and sat in the same class for eight years. He was my companion in many school competitions and sports teams. We had known each other too long and too well to keep up pretences.

I was still under the strong impression of the previous day when I said, "I can't believe we behave like enemies. Is this the way we will relate to one another from now on?"

"You know what I worry about the most?" he said. "That one day, when this isolation is way behind us, I don't think we'll even remember what we used to think and see as normal. Our lives and mindsets will be reshaped into something different, who knows what." I feared the same.

My friend and I spent our youth in the atmosphere of war and its aftermath, when our society was destroyed and re-formed in a short time. For a whole decade, people struggled to find their way out of the mess and confusion so they could take back control over their lives. They resized and readjusted their routines, carrying on in hope that the good old days would come around again.

Even though my friend and I were only young teenagers when the war started, we were also nostalgic about the way things used to be.

When I started going to school, being a straight-A student was a thing of pride. My class was frequently the strongest within our year and even within the entire school. The bar was always set high, and we competed with one another just to see who could do more or do better.

We were raised to believe in the power of knowledge. Teachers, community leaders, and role models were experts in their fields. So many TV shows during my upbringing spread the message that it was better to know useless things than to remain ignorant.

My environment was also set up to support progress. My sister would sit for hours at the dining room table and practise math under the supervision of my father. Mom helped me draw animals for my science and art class, and we often rehearsed poems I had to know by heart.

Dad only assisted me with STEM projects (Science, Technology, Engineering and Mathematics). I had to make coasters out of plywood and some geometric shapes out of metal. I didn't know how to properly use the tools when in class, and he borrowed some from his workplace so I could finish my models at home.

He never missed an opportunity to check how well I knew basic technical principles. Even a completely ordinary situation was a chance for him to give me a math task and check whether I was technically literate or not.

"That's more important than you assume," he insisted. For him, it basically meant that my head wasn't completely empty, and that I was ready for life in the twentieth century.

I remember a time when I was twelve or thirteen, when I called out to my dad to come help me. Even though I interrupted his precious TV time, he didn't mind.

"What're you doing?" he said, looking at my hands.

"I'm making a cake and I was going to use this dish." I showed him a deeper dish than my mom usually used. "She puts in less eggs and flour because she's cooking for the five of us. But now I am expecting more people to come over. Do you think this one will be big enough?" I couldn't make up my mind, so I wanted to hear his opinion.

He replied the way he always did. "Use your brain and you'll get the answer." He was convinced he was helping me when a few seconds later he added, "Don't you see that the dish is shaped like a cylinder? You know how to calculate the volume of a cylinder: $V=\pi r^2 h$. Grab a piece of paper and work it out."

I wanted to laugh, but I rolled my eyes instead. I watched him jump out of his armchair, all fired up. He picked up a piece of paper and a pencil, determined to show me how to solve this problem. He explained the process step by step while I stood next to him, nodding.

Even though at that moment I promised myself I'd never ask him anything ever again, I was at the same time amazed at how much he knew and how much effort he put into explaining it all to me.

The most interesting part, however, was the end of these crash courses. He would always ask me the same questions he somehow never knew the answers to.

"Which grade are you in, again? Are you learning physics now? How did you do on your last math test?" And he questioned whether my math teacher was doing her job properly because I didn't know something that was so apparent to him.

That mindset changed just a few years later, when the new conditions and life circumstances altered our approach to everything, including education. Many of my friends wanted to pursue studies but had to give up and start earning a living. Others relied on their parents' or relatives' promises that they'd be taken care of. All they had to do was enrol in courses that were in demand and save themselves from survival fears. I belonged to a third group, which was the smallest, and decided to follow my personal interests. But that choice came at a high cost.

I felt as if I was taking part in a real-life version of a famous Yugoslavian quiz show from the 1980s, called *Kviskoteka*.[50] Participants competed in many different disciplines, all of which were interesting. The detective game was the one I would never miss. I

---

50 Quiz show broadcast by TV Zagreb, Croatia between 1980 and 1995. Some of the games were: ABCD Riddles, Association Game, Detection Game, and Question and Answer Game.

always listened carefully and tried my best to figure out the mystery person.

Three guests would get up on stage and read their name, surname, and profession. They were, of course, the same for all, but only one of those three people was telling the truth. The contestants had to figure out which one it was.

The key difference between this quiz and our real-life game was that none of the mystery guests evoked any interest. No one wanted to hear who they were. Quite the opposite: they, as well as I, were now in the hot seat.

I was made to believe that everything I was and did was wrong. Whenever I tried to explain myself or share my views, no one would listen. It was as if I was the mysterious guest and would only repeat:

Person A: I'm completely mad, but I'm choosing to pursue my own path.

Person B: I'm completely mad, but I'm choosing to pursue my own path.

Person C: I'm completely mad, but I'm choosing to pursue my own path.

"How are you going to survive?" some questioned my reality. "What kind of a fairy tale do you think you live in?" others mocked. "No one on Earth cares anymore about what you know or what kind of person you are; why would you do so?" Some of them could swear I was that way because I was carefree and spoilt. "It is easy for you to work on yourself when you are privileged," I heard them concluding. Gosh, how wrong they were!

For years, I was constantly trying to determine what normal really meant. Who would I consider normal? My countrymen battled through daily lives anesthetised by images of violence and suffering. All we saw on TV was mixed up scenes of horror and the pretence that it wasn't happening. On one side was news about war crime, inflation, corruption, scandals, and losses; and on the other, songs of an easy life and eternal peace and joy. Anything in between, anything I would have thought of as normal, didn't exist.

Survival was the only life we knew. And that life was merciless, full of evil and carelessness. Self-interest sprang up like a weed; lies and shame became weapons used to control others. All success, power, or achievements were there to show others what they didn't and couldn't have.

I struggled against this way of looking at life and tried to understand why it had to be that way. I attributed it at first to the effects of the war and the impoverishment of the country. But after some time, it became clearer and clearer to me I was deceiving myself. "It has always been this way and it will always be," I heard people say. I began to see those sad power games everywhere I looked: in books I read, in my family lineage, in front of me in its most shameless version. Every single day.

At that time, the more powerful people rushed to set themselves apart and act out their new roles. I couldn't decide which group I found more repulsive. Perhaps those who focused solely on amassing material things. Through money, they gained self-respect and a feeling of success and importance. They bragged about the convenience of their VIP lives and tried to convince me that everything in this world, including existence itself, came down to economics.

But there were also other types of players who taught themselves to be the cream of the crop. After spending a childhood in socialism and an atmosphere of togetherness, I was unprepared to face so much arrogance and snobbery. It seemed many could barely wait to publicly show off their ancestry or status. They would boast by mentioning names of their eminent ancestors or postal codes. Without any effort or achievement, they considered themselves influential, and I, not being from the same litter, had to question the right to call myself human.

I was so disappointed with people. "It doesn't have to be this way," I often said. I tortured both myself and others with various questions and statements. "We already went through war; do we have to continue belittling each other? Where is the reality in which life isn't some kind of menagerie? Where are people who don't immediately force others into these boxes of winners and vanquished?"

I pushed back angrily against my society. I didn't want to accept a single role it assigned. No one could tell me what I had to do, think, or say. I didn't want anyone to explain to me how things stood or how I was to live my life.

"No!" was my only and final answer to all societal requests. My life was already small and crazy, and I didn't plan to make it completely meaningless.

Anybody who accepted those social and economic conditions seemed wrong to me. I criticized my family members or friends for being weak, blind, and obedient. I called them out as liars or accused them of being enablers. "You disgust me!" I repeated over and over again.

But the more I resisted, the stronger the pressure grew. It pushed deeper into my personal space and tried to twist my experience of reality. I was told I'd see life clearly once I got my head out of my books. They emphasized that because I was a woman, I didn't have the choices and freedom I thought I had. Women in my society, I heard, never achieved anything without the support of men. I had to give up on myself or I wouldn't get far. I had to be quiet, find protection, and put up with my life as it was. They told me the fulfilment I looked for didn't exist.

Despite my resistance, I went through long periods of self-doubt and second-guessing myself. Maybe the people who were telling me I was the problem were indeed right? Did the world I kept talking about exist anywhere? I found only a few like-minded people, and they were on the brink of losing hope for a better life.

Every time I thought about the future, my stomach got tied up in knots. What was I going to do after I finished college? Setting new goals didn't make any sense. Why would I put my time and energy into something that wasn't worth striving for? I couldn't see my place in the world around me. Instead of following my father's steps, who never looked back or regretted the sacrifices he had made in the name of the future he wished to live, I became depressed. I didn't care for tomorrow.

I cut myself off from others without even thinking about whether I was being harsh or unfair towards them. Overwhelmed by my own pain, I searched for a way to soothe it. Books and exams were my only sacred space in a stream of long years, the only sense of peace and progress. Everything else was just a repetition of the same aimless day. I felt like I was living in a trap.

I learned to look at my surroundings like a stranger might. I told myself I was, for some reason, cursed to be born on this meridian. Somewhere out there must be a different world. I used that belief to entertain my friends and make fun of myself. "I am actually perfect, did you know that, but the trick is I have to find the place where I can be myself."

The truth was, I knew nothing about the world outside my country. Until then, I'd only travelled once, on a school trip. No one from my close family or friends had ever lived overseas. I knew some people who left the country, but they managed it because of their status as refugees and with the help of international organizations. I wasn't in their position, so I didn't know where to begin.

I had all sorts of questions. Where would I go? Could I do it alone? Where would I get the money? What would I do once I got there? I didn't have anybody to talk to. And when I would ask or speak up, I was met with silence or incomprehensible judgement. Dragged down by all the uncertainty I'd already experienced, I became anxious. I wondered if my plan had any chance of turning out well.

But then, just like in the movies, life made a turn for me. I had given up watching the news many years before and wasn't up to date on everything that was happening in my country. On the evening of March 24, 1999, I was ironing in the living room, while Dad napped on the couch with our dog, Dora. It was just the three of us, as my mom, sister, and brother had gone out.

The telephone rang. I was greeted by a family friend with whom I immediately started chatting. I told him about recently passing my exam and about the party I'd been to the previous weekend. He was quiet, more than usual, and asked me to get my brother and sister to call him when they returned. He needed to know we were all okay. It sounded so strange, and I couldn't help asking him what it was all about.

"Promise me you won't be scared," he said and then he brought up something about bombs. I didn't react because I didn't understand what he was talking about.

Right at that moment, sirens rang out. "What is happening?" I raised my voice, trying to connect with him. The noise was overwhelming; I could hear him saying something, but I didn't understand a word. The phone was still in my hand, while thoughts were flying through my head. Should I hang up? Should I stay on the line? Where was this sound coming from and why? Completely muddled, I hung up; the noise was gone. It was again quiet in the apartment. I wondered what it was and got up from the stool. I took a step towards the living room and BOOM, a crash shook the entire building. Instinctively, I spread my hands and pressed them against the wall in the hallway, screaming.

In a few seconds, scenes changed right in front of my eyes. I first saw the dog jump from the couch and run towards the bathroom. Then my dad woke up, whining about the noise he thought I'd made.

"Don't tell me you dropped the iron on the floor. I don't understand you kids anymore, what's got into you?" He was still complaining about the iron my sister had accidentally destroyed a few weeks earlier. We had finally bought a new one, and his first thought upon waking was that I'd ruined this one too.

"It's not me!" I yelled, checking the channels on our TV. Finally, on one that was broadcasting an old movie, *Battle of Kosovo*,[51] along the bottom of the screen was a sentence: NATO was bombing us. After decades of animosity between Albanians and Serbs from the Kosovo[52] region, hostility had escalated to the point of no return. Serbia was now a war zone.

I was shocked. My dad looked through me and asked what I'd just said. He must have still been half asleep.

Surprisingly, in those first few minutes we didn't panic. When I watched movies about bombing, I would always see people rushing through houses, calling for family members or neighbours. It was always messy and scary. But in our case, maybe because it was still unbelievable, it wasn't like that. We acted almost normal. I checked to ensure I had turned off the iron and hurried to the bathroom to find my dog. She was shaking alone in the dark. I got down on my knees and

---

[51] A 1989 Yugoslav film directed by Zdravko Šotra. The film marked the 600th anniversary of the historical battle between Serbs and Turks at Kosovo. The 1389 battle incurred losses on both sides, including both leaders and much of the Serbian nobility. Seventy years later, Serbia became part of the Ottoman Empire.

[52] In 1999, Kosovo was part of Serbia, but became an independent country in 2008. Kosovo plays an important role in Serbian identity; it was the birthplace of the Serbian Orthodox Church in the Middle Ages, and a part of the most powerful Serbian state. Between the 15th and beginning of the 20th century, Kosovo had been part of the Ottoman Empire. This conquest changed its demographic and identity, and deep-rooted tensions between Christians and Muslims persist to this day.

brought her closer to my chest. "Don't worry. You'll be fine," I said. I think I was also trying to reassure myself.

In the next fifteen minutes, one by one, my mom, my sister, and my brother came back to the apartment. Mom mentioned drinking coffee with a neighbour when that bomb went off. My sister was with her boyfriend, and my brother thought it was an earthquake. He was driving back home from another part of town, which wasn't hit in the first attack. He didn't understand why people were rushing out from the buildings.

"Whole communities were on the street," he said. "I didn't even think it was a bombing." The whole chaotic scene came with the same question: was this real or not? No one could easily accept the fact that it was.

Dad and I found one radio station which was giving information on what to do. Our neighbourhood was built in the late 1970s, and we had a huge underground bomb shelter. We were told to hide there and wait for a new siren to announce the end of the danger. My sister and I did so, spending the next couple of hours down there.

Over the next two or three weeks, I went to the shelter a few more times with my childhood girlfriend. Some people weren't leaving the safe place, especially the elderly and families with infants. The shelter was filled with chairs, improvised beds, blankets, electric burners, and so on. I heard there should be a restroom down there, but I didn't see one. I only remember seeing some men cleaning buckets people used as toilets.

I stopped going to the shelter for a few reasons. Firstly, there wasn't a military base or any buildings of strategic significance in my neighbourhood, which meant we were a bit safer than some of my fellow citizens. Secondly, pets were not allowed into the shelters, and people were split between those who agreed and those who objected to that rule. I was in the second group, and I felt for people who had lost their pets to heart attacks during the NATO bombing. Thirdly, I had a flashback while spending one late evening in the shelter. My high school classmate, who fled Sarajevo at the beginning of the civil war, spent years grieving for the life she had before coming to Belgrade. I listened to her talk about every detail of her old days and what she would do if she would get the chance to live that life again. She made me promise one thing. I thought it was crazy back then, but she insisted so hard that I gave in.

"If you ever experience bombing in your city," she said, "give me your word you will face your death ready. Wear your best clothes and put your dearest belongings of your current life in a backpack. That's all you'll have with you, forever."

I knew about the VHS tape she'd hidden in an armchair because her parents didn't approve of her watching the movie *Hair*.[53] And I also learned about the new jacket she was hoping to wear after spring break in 1992. "If no one knows who you are, you'll know. You'll see it." I watched as she struggled with identity loss and even how she wished she'd died in Sarajevo.

One evening, in April 1999, I went to the shelter. I wore my best clothes and had a backpack full of memories with me. Although I laughed and listened to my childhood friend tease me about my outfit, I was honest with myself: I didn't want to survive. I imagined my city destroyed and concluded I didn't have enough strength or hope for one more round of hell. I'd already forgotten my happy childhood years and felt as if they weren't ever part of my life experience. All I knew was an existence full of uncertainty, loss, and pain, and I was tired of it.

During the days when we had electricity, instead of studying, I started to make a cookbook. As a kid I wasn't ever into food, and even resisted showing up in the kitchen and learning more about it. Now, for some reason, I wanted to collect all the recipes I liked. My friends thought I was nuts when they shared their favourite recipes over the phone.

---

53 An American anti-war musical drama based on a successful Broadway musical; the film was directed by Miloš Forman in 1979. A young man from Oklahoma goes to New York to join the US army during the Vietnam War. He meets a group of hippies in Central Park and falls in love with a city girl. The group want to keep the couple together and safe.

"What are you going to do with them?" I honestly couldn't give a proper answer. But years later, when I was much older and different from that resentful young woman, it crossed my mind that I was actually saying goodbye while filling my backpack with the things I called mine. Food reminded me of many great events and dear people from my extended family and my country of origin. In years to come, food would also help me build a bridge to many beautiful friendships and moments I shared with people from all over the world.

Two months into the bombing, in May 1999, I packed my things and headed overseas with my sister. Many pieces of my life situation at that time made this chapter possible. My brother refused to go into the army in February that year. He said he didn't want to die for someone else's interests. My parents were understanding of his decision, especially when they watched our neighbours trying to get any information about their sons in the army. Even today, I remember a note I read on the front door of a local library. "I won't be working anytime soon. I went to get my boy back home."

After forty years of working, my dad went into a well-deserved retirement that winter, and by law, he had to wait six months for his first pension. We were running out of money as my sister and mother had stopped going to work in April. It wasn't safe anymore to stay inside the government buildings. Most of the stores were closed, and staff had been sent home.

TOXICITY AND DISCONNECTION

Everything around me sank deeper into chaos and fear as normal life was reduced to breaks between sirens, shelters, and news of more deaths.

My sister and I went out one night to walk along the Danube riverbank, and a girlfriend she knew showed up. She was getting ready to leave the country, which I thought was impossible. But I was wrong. While she was talking, I exchanged a glance with my sister.

Later, I told her we should go too. Her friend had given us an idea of where we could go and how we could arrange the trip.

In the next few days, we gathered more information about flights, about the country we were heading to, and the cost of living. Some of our fellow citizens were already there, and we got in contact with one woman through a mutual friend. We started packing. I borrowed money from a friend and informed my closest friends we were leaving. We didn't tell our parents, as we knew they would try to stop us. They had a good reason to do so. We were all together, all safe, and with a roof over our heads.

While my sister and I searched for an opportunity to tell them, it appeared of its own accord and exploded like that first bomb. A woman from JAT[54] called our home number, and my mom

---

54   Yugoslav Airways was founded in 1927 as Aeroput. In 1947, JAT became the national flag carrier in Yugoslavia, and later Serbia. In 2013, JAT Airways became Air of Serbia.

picked up the phone. The departure time for the bus which would take us out of the country had changed unexpectedly, and she wanted to let us know. When we arrived at the front door of the apartment that night, Mom had a nitroglycerin tablet in her mouth and Dad was calming her down.

The conversation went back and forth. I told them I couldn't live this way anymore. I didn't want to be talked out of leaving.

"There is no better solution," I said. I was firm and told them it didn't matter what they said or did. I had made up my mind, and we were leaving. When my mom saw I couldn't be dissuaded, she turned to my father, expecting he would force me to stay.

"Don't just stand there. Do something!" she yelled. In some other situations I would have listened to him, but in that moment I didn't care.

"I can't take it any longer. I'm tired of feeling helpless," I cried. "If I don't go, I will die inside."

He cut the drama off when he understood I would not back down. "Tell me the details," he said. I told him what plans I did have and about other things that needed to be sorted out.

We cried that night. I was so scared, but knowing I was leaving the madness helped chase away my fears. I needed to go, and I needed to go now.

CHAPTER NINE

Somewhere in Between

My journey began at one of the Belgrade city squares. Slavija is usually very busy, as many bus and tram lines cross their paths there, but that May morning it was eerily quiet and empty. The only signs of life were at the point where our bus stopped, which was in front of the nearby hotel.

We arrived a bit early to ensure we didn't miss the bus, and also to say goodbye to our friends. Quite a few showed up, arriving from all corners of the city. Most friends came by bus or by car, while one rode his bike for a few kilometres. He had to cross one bridge, which wouldn't be worth mentioning, except that city bridges were a target of NATO bombings. No one knew which one would be next.

I didn't sleep well the night before. I was so restless thinking about what would happen to all of us. Seeing my friends at the bus stop gave me hope for a moment – hope that everything would be all right. But in the next moment I was furious that life was the way it was.

"Call me when you cross the border," one girlfriend said. "Call anybody, just so that we all know you've made it over." In those days, NATO had military operations in the eastern part of Serbia, which was the route we took to leave the country. My friends exchanged phone numbers so they could stay in touch later.

"Don't worry," I said, but we all did anyway. Back then, I couldn't help myself; I openly cursed my country and how things were. I did regret it later; I'd been unaware of how much my words were disheartening and even insulting to some of my friends.

The bus took off on time, and we were on our way to the Bulgaria[55] airport. In any other situation, I would have said we had a pleasant ride, because it passed without any problems. But maybe it is better to say it was safe. We only stopped once in Serbia for a short break and went on to the Bulgarian border. There were no signs of airplanes or military on the road, nor any problems with customs.

It was during those hours when I thought the most about the uncertainty my sister and I faced. We were truly fleeing. I didn't know the country I was going to or what I would do there. I had never lived

---

55 A country situated in Southeast Europe, in the east of the Balkans.

on my own, never paid a bill or rent, and if you didn't count my graduation trip, I had never been abroad. It was such a strange feeling to travel in that space in between, not knowing how things would unfold at both ends.

My sister and I didn't talk too much. We focused blindly on the steps we had to take to reach Cyprus:[56] get out of Serbia, cross the border with Bulgaria, get to the airport in Sofia,[57] and board our flight to Limassol.[58] We rushed towards those marked points, quickly jumping from one to another, not allowing anything to slow us down.

We spent just a few hours in Bulgaria, mostly at the airport, and that part of the trip remains somewhat blurry. When we landed in Cyprus, the official at the airport told us we had to fill out a form before we entered the country. He told us to make sure not to leave a single field blank. Then he gestured towards a table with enough space for a few passengers.

I scanned the paper and realized we didn't have an address in the country we had entered. That line was marked with a red star, which meant it was mandatory. On the other side of the airport, a woman from Belgrade waited for us. She was a friend of my

---

56 The Republic of Cyprus is an island country, the third largest and third most populous island in the Mediterranean.
57 The capital and the largest city in Bulgaria.
58 A city on the southern coast of Cyprus, the second largest and popular tourist destination.

sister's friend, and we had spoken with her over the phone. Although we got a lot of information from her, we'd forgotten to ask for her address.

For a moment, I tried to figure out what we should do. I looked around and instinctively hurried to one of the tables. Two minutes later, I sat back down with my sister.

"Here, I'm done." She looked at me in disbelief. She was also trying to think of a way to solve our problem.

"You're joking." She took my form and glanced at it, searching for the address. "Where'd you find it?" She was stunned.

"I copied it from that guy who was standing next to me. He's from here; I heard him speaking their language. I put the next house number. We just have to be careful not to go to the same customs officer as him." My heart beat faster, even though I appeared in control. I didn't want to think about breaking the law or the consequences I could face. I just wanted to get to the other side, and nothing could stop me.

I entered this new space without any guidance. As I went from situation to situation, the many fears I'd brought with me dissolved, and I paved my own path.

The fake address worked. My sister and I received refugee status, and with it, the right to legally stay in Cyprus. The young woman who waited for us had already rented an apartment and offered her unconditional support. Many of my fellow countrymen and women were already there, which helped us feel less alone and isolated. We were all in the same boat, looking for the same answers, so we shared every piece of information we gathered on the way.

The first thing I did was look for a job, and I found one. I am not sure why Serbs had special treatment regarding employment. Maybe it was because of the bombing or because Cypriots had a close connection with my country of origin. Many doors stayed open, and everything was a lot easier than I'd anticipated. Nobody asked for my resume or asked about a working visa. I did any job I felt I could accept, and that brought me the money I needed to survive. I worked in a café, then in a hotel, and later as a tour guide.

My new surroundings and daily responsibilities engrossed me. I was carried away by their demands and challenges. I didn't think much about getting my papers in order. I childishly avoided even talking about it or being reminded of my situation. I wanted to believe it would work out on its own.

Cyprus helped me escape into a space where I felt out of reach and safer than ever before in my adult life. The whole environment was warm and welcoming. I could smell the scent of early summer in the air and enjoyed its uplifting energy. The presence of the beautiful Mediterranean Sea enhanced my feeling of ease and peacefulness, which was something I had longed for. We arrived in the middle of the season and found Limassol bursting at the seams. There were thousands of tourists from almost all parts of the world. They poured down the streets, bringing the sounds of different languages, and different facial expressions. With a word or two, via a book or a drawing given as a gift, I could easily connect with them.

I was overwhelmed by this change. It fluttered before me like a colourful New Year's display in a shop window. It was such a stark contrast to the frozen and darkened image I carried inside myself. In Cyprus, there was no place for the experience of death and thoughts of powerlessness. I thought I was in heaven.

A massive weight lifted off my shoulders, and I felt a wind propelling me forward. The smile returned to my face. I made new friends, I came across individuals who helped me, I fell in love, my health stabilized. All I wanted was to embrace every chance – even the slightest one – to engage with the world around me. For a few months, I was actually living another life and experiencing what I hadn't for almost a decade.

I needed years after to understand why I couldn't let go of this chapter of my life. For the first time, I had found a space wide enough for both my intuition and abilities, and also for my ignorance and mistakes. I was truly young.

The bombing ended on June 10, 1999, which affected our status on the island. I heard more often that we now had to have a visa to stay and work legally. It became obvious we would have to make some hard choices. My sister decided to go home, as she was sure this adventure wasn't something she wanted for herself.

I was in a state of mind where I constantly went back and forth, remaining always somewhere in between. I wasn't aware that I had become accustomed to this state of being over the course of the 90s, as it was my way of coping with my life circumstances. I wanted parts of both lives: to finish my studies, get a degree, and rely on myself, but also to live my love story and remain outside of the chaos and toxicity of my broken society.

Late in the summer, I got a phone call from my girlfriend in Belgrade who asked me to be her maid of honour at her wedding. She planned to get married in October, and she needed to know if I would return by then. I thought it would be nice to be part of such a great occasion. Maybe I could pass my exam, I hoped, and then come back. I wanted to believe it would be doable and said yes. I envisioned nothing less than a fairy tale.

Things were quite different. I left Cyprus in tears and heartbroken.

The first weeks after I returned to Belgrade went by very quickly because I had a lot going on. I caught up with my friends, was maid of honour at the wedding, took an exam, and enrolled in my fourth year of university. I fluttered around, half-living in Serbia, half in Cyprus, not wanting to face reality. I would run to internet cafés to get in touch with my friends on the island, or call or write to reconnect. It didn't get me anywhere. I comfortlessly cried for months as I finally realized that I wasn't going back.

But I didn't want to be home either. Cyprus had changed me. No matter which way I turned, I kept running into the person I didn't feel was me anymore. As though years had passed since I'd left, I couldn't relate to my old world.

I was reliant on my parents, which I now experienced as imprisonment. I was more impatient with people and refused to buy into the story of waiting for things to change so we could begin living normally again. I knew that day wasn't coming. At least not for me. I felt trapped.

Soon, the only thing I thought about was leaving again. But now I knew what living abroad really meant and was more realistic about the demands of a life I had to build from scratch. I tried to share my uncertainties with some friends, but we got tangled into misunderstandings. On one side, there was me trying to explain all the intricacies of my life, and on the other, silence. It was as if I was describing some unknown galaxy. I constantly felt unheard and, in a sense, rejected. Because they couldn't keep up with the new me, my friends felt judged and avoided communicating. I was pushed further into a state of isolation.

My family also had different opinions on my life views, especially regarding my decision to live abroad. While my dad gave me the freedom to make my own choice and only expected me to be responsible for my life and well-being, my mom and sister criticized me often.

"Life is the same everywhere," my sister said. She hurried to share stories about people who had returned to the country, saying that Serbia was the only home in the world. Mom wanted me to accept reality as it was, to work tomorrow in a school and have what she thought of as a normal life.

"Why don't you live like all the other good kids do?" she asked. Then she would blame herself for making mistakes during my upbringing.

I turned to books as I had done years before, just to find change slipped into this space too. I continued to study with interest, but I no longer saw nor searched for shelter in my reading. In fact, I longed to get out, and I perceived my studies as something that held me back. That's how I started to play difficult, unfair, and unnecessary games with myself. When it came to my exams, I was still as responsible and dedicated as before, but the moment they were done, I plucked every connection to them out of my head. I associated reading books with staying in the country and a reality I now knew I didn't want to live in. I would then say all I wanted was a diploma, which would help me apply more easily for immigration.

After a decade of various forms of violence and scarcity, my country was in a state of change. In the year 2000, political systems shifted, and a wave of optimism swept over people. I'll never forget a scene from the local hair salon. I needed my highlights done, so I called my hairdresser to book an appointment. No one answered for several hours; in the late afternoon, I took my dog and walked to the salon.

It was full of women all talking excitedly. The atmosphere was one that usually precedes a night out.

"What's happening?" I asked my stylist when I got closer. "I've been trying to call you for hours," I said.

"I'm sorry, I haven't had time to answer the phone. Look," she gestured to a salon full of girls, "it's been like this for a few days now. My guess is that people kept their money under their mattresses and waited to spend it on a special occasion." She was referring to the mass celebration downtown to mark the new political change. "Now everybody's rushing to get their hair done."

A woman who sat on a chair shared her feelings with me. "Somehow, I feel I can fully breathe! Things will be better from now on, don't you think?" Her voice was excited and high-pitched. I didn't say anything, just smiled.

I left the salon and came across a friend in a passageway. I asked her how she was doing, but all she wanted to talk about was politics.

She talked about the new government. "I'm giving them two years to sort out this chaos." She was referring to the war, isolation, and bombing. "It'll be just like it was before, you'll see." She was also certain of a happy ending.

I nodded my head. I did not see any point in sharing my negativity. I had done that for years, and it brought nothing but conflict.

The euphoria of my compatriots hadn't touched me at all. I felt the same and thought the same. I was not planning to stay, so these changes didn't matter much to me.

But I still didn't know where I would go after graduation and how I would get there.

Two years later, I got an opportunity to visit an old friend who now lived in the USA. It was post 9/11, and it took weeks of personal and background evaluation before I received my month-long tourist visa. When I got a phone call from the embassy, I remember rushing downtown and picking up my passport in front of the building. No one was allowed to go in. I stood in a small group along with some elderly couples whose children were US citizens. We were the lucky ones, as most of the applications were denied.

This second experience of living abroad had many similarities to the first one. It was as if I'd shed my old skin after I crossed the border. In this new place, I became a new me and easily connected with strangers.

In the USA, I had a host and didn't have to worry about survival, so I freely explored new cultures. As always, I was interested to hear how people lived and wanted to understand their mindsets, life goals, and dreams. Using every opportunity I could to communicate, I made friends with some of my neighbours, and the staff and members of the local library. I also helped at the nursery at a local Greek Church.

But something was very different. My host was closely related to people who came from various parts of my former country of Yugoslavia. Although most of them were younger than me, which meant they were children at the beginning of the war, their families had gone through painful life experiences and had a lot of trauma to process. Until then, I'd believed that leaving the country was a sure way to escape the madness of our war and post-war reality. I came to understand that running thousands of kilometres away from home didn't bring peace or freedom from the horrors and fears left behind.

It seemed there was only one truth. No one truly comprehended what they'd brought with them before they started unpacking it. It became visible mostly in the way they interpreted new life paths and experiences. Everything was seen through the lens of the old life.

I spoke with a young woman who couldn't settle down in her new home. She went from job to job, not staying in any place too long. While I found this attitude admirable, because it was a way to discover and learn about new things, I couldn't understand why she wasn't into digging and finding something she was really good at. Usually when I said things like this, I got a lot of pushback. People rolled their eyes and criticized me for being naive.

But I'd always supported people in following their interests, maybe because from an early age I'd known many who did what they loved. I admired the passion and strength with which they welcomed every new work challenge, and I also enjoyed seeing how their self-motivation kept them moving forward. They always believed the best was yet to come.

I made this woman angry when I mentioned this.

"To work at what I love? And what's the future of it?" she asked.

By the tone of her voice, I could tell I had crossed a line and gone into forbidden territory, so I remained quiet.

"I don't want to end up like my mother. She dedicated herself to one profession, and when the war started, she managed to keep her job but at a high cost. She put up with every humiliation because she feared we would end up on the streets!" Then she came to the main point. "Not me. I will be ready. I don't want to close myself off to other options and then find myself stuck in a situation I can't get out of."

Our conversation ended there, but those words stayed with me for a long time. They touched the most vulnerable spot within me, one I rarely spoke about. I knew she was trying to protect herself from feeling helpless and dependent on people she couldn't trust. Although I hadn't lost even a fraction of the things she had, I understood that sense of insecurity. That was how I had experienced life in an isolated country, a walled-off city, barriers between and within people, cruelty, the lack of resources, and the broken system of social and personal values.

I spent six months in America, longer than I'd initially planned, which was enough to redirect myself and open a few new chapters upon my return to Serbia. I took two major steps into independence. I finally finished university and started working. Also, I wasn't alone anymore, as I found a partner who shared both my personal and professional responsibilities.

I stuck with my decision not to follow the career of teaching. I willingly engaged in a completely new occupation: information technology (IT). It was something my partner did for a living, and because he was originally from Croatia, now living in Serbia, self-employment became his and our best career option. We continued our lives as a married couple and a team.

This phase was a time when I understood how distanced I had become from my surroundings. The business world made it even clearer to me. I simply couldn't find my way and doubted I ever could. I came across people who shared the same values and had spent a few decades struggling to keep their integrity in check. While my generation was in their late twenties and dreamed of proving themselves and creating something fresh, the older generations remained disheartened and focused on their own issues.

I was getting close to thirty, a time when people usually feel an urge to set up a new stage and take on real life responsibilities. I knew I had to rethink my current situation and decide on my future. I had an open discussion with my husband.

"I'm sick of this mess. I try every day not to hear the things I learned about. I repress so many unwanted truths about my society, but I still see them, and they bother me. My spirit is dragged down by every life circumstance and crushed by the thought this reality won't ever change. I've tried to reconnect and participate; God knows I've tried. But it isn't working. The worst part is that I'm not motivated by any goal. Even the thought of making it to the top doesn't excite me. This isn't me." I said it all without any bitterness, and I calmly added, "I've come back twice to my country, and I finished what I wanted to. Now it's time to go."

"I'm with you," he said. His reaction told me we were on the same page. It was such a relief since I'd found little support from my family and most of my friends.

Neither he nor I had any illusions about what life was like overseas. Before we met, he took some certification courses and spent almost two years living between Britain and Croatia. Moving to Serbia also brought a lot of life challenges and required many personal adjustments from his side.

We took the time to look at the immigration opportunities and weigh our options as we opened ourselves to new information. Soon after, we crossed paths with a couple who had applied for immigration to Canada, and their example inspired us to do the same.

Our wish was to move as soon as possible, so we acted promptly and applied to one of the programs. But life had another plan that brought a twist into my story, one I never thought I'd write about.

The immigration process changed due to political shifts in Canada, and our application was put on hold for a time. Instead of starting a new life far away, which we thought would happen in just a matter of weeks, we ended up staying in Croatia. We had only come for a short stay in the spring of 2007. Now we had to live there.

If someone had told me during the 1990s that I would live in Zagreb after the war, I would've never believed them. I remember thinking back then that someone should build concrete walls on the borders and restrain us from any future interactions. What's the point of building connections if they sooner or later bring us to the same old animosities and new tragedies? After the war, Serbs who were born in Croatia, and those whose families had lived there for generations, weren't welcome, let alone a Serb from Serbia. In my wildest dreams, I wouldn't have taken the smallest step into a zone so full of prejudices, unresolved trauma, and life uncertainty.

However, our new start in Zagreb had many favourable advantages. From the beginning, we had support from my in-laws. My husband was able to continue his career, and I found a lot of similarities between our societies. I knew the language, I could drive a car with my Serbian driver's licence and, to my surprise I learned about the existence of a private Serbian high school. Despite my huge inner resistance and my wish to do anything but a job that would take me back to my earlier life, I took a teaching job there.

Day by day, not knowing when or if we would ever be able to complete our immigration process, my husband and I built our new life and lived the best we could. There were months and months in which I wouldn't think about leaving, especially as I got deeply involved in my work at the school. But then, I also had periods of immense distress when I cried and cried over the uncertainty and what I experienced as a constant entrapment in a life somewhere in between.

What I appreciated the most in my new life, and what kept me going forward, was the small community of people I kept close to my heart. My new friends accepted and motivated me, which was funny because that was exactly what they credited me for.

"You're a mystery to us," they said. They never once assumed their presence helped me solve what I used to think was the biggest mystery in my life.

It began when I noticed they all behaved the same way, which I couldn't understand at the beginning. They all had different affinities and professions. There was so much variety in their family histories and the environments and circumstances they had grown up with, but then again, it was as if they were all repeating one, and only one, pattern of life. Beneath the surface, they all struggled with a debilitating lack of trust. Trust in people, in the future, in life in general.

I shortly understood this was exactly what brought us together. Without realizing it, we behaved as though we were lab rats, programmed to follow the same route over and over. One step forward, two steps back. Never turning our backs for too long, because as we all knew, sooner or later the darkness would creep in and take away everything we had. We never had enough faith to relax and flow with what life was bringing our way.

Some of my friends were deeply affected by the circumstances they grew up in. They were teenagers during the war, at a time when violence and hopelessness were the only reality they knew. When they were children, they saw adults losing their ground and being frightened for their very survival. The trauma imprinted into their minds and souls, leaving them with the impression that the only expected things in life were deception, shock, and derailment.

Full of tension, they sensed new danger behind every moment of ease. "I know what you are," they seemed to say to life itself. "But this time I will be prepared for your arrival. The price of ignorance is too high." They didn't want to be swept away and become just another one of those people who, having suddenly become obsolete, remained superfluous forever.

Years passed, and my friends had the impression they were participating in life. But the truth was, they didn't contribute half as much as they could. They reminded me of some of my childhood friends who had never found any satisfaction in the games we played. Instead, they remained stuck in a place with no joy, controlled by an overwhelming and all-consuming fear of the ball.

Some were so used to retreating they couldn't recognize the moment when they were offered the freedom to make a better choice.

One evening, I was waiting for my husband to finish using the computer. I needed to talk to him, so I interrupted his work.

"Are you doing something important?" I asked. "Let's take a walk. If we don't go now, it'll be dark soon."

"I'm making a travel itinerary for this young guy at work. He wants to go to London," he told me as he looked up from the screen.

"He could take me with him." I sat down at the table, interested in the topic. I had never been to London, although I always wanted to go. "So, does he need a visa?" For decades, this was the first question I asked. In my reality, a visa was an insurmountable obstacle only some could pass.

"Nope. He just needs two things: an approval for vacation from his manager and some money," he answered as he sorted through some papers.

"He has a job and a monthly paycheque, right? He lives with his parents?" I asked while checking these facts off a list in my head, as if they were questions from some well-known survey.

"Yes, he lives with his mother, but I know where you are heading. It's not all about the money. He can afford it," my husband said. "He's never been outside of Croatia, and he desperately wants to drink a beer in a real British pub." This reason in itself wouldn't be enough to motivate me to go to London, but I understood it.

While my husband was leafing through his papers, he told me how this young guy had come up to him at lunchtime and asked him how we managed to travel so often. Where did we get the money, when it's so expensive to buy tickets, to pay for hotels and food, and to rent a vehicle? My husband assured him it wasn't impossible. He could make use of the options available to all European youngsters: cheaper flights, hostels, public transport passes. He could also choose to go during the off-season or to a destination that was not currently popular, in order to save money for food and city exploration.

While living in Croatia, we travelled through European countries, planning ahead of time how we could get the most out of our trip. With two regular jobs and fewer visa requirements for me, we made trips I could only have dreamed of when I lived in Serbia. We went to Hungary, Italy, Austria, Sweden, Czech Republic, Cyprus, and Slovenia.

But I knew it wasn't easy to liberate yourself from the world I used to refer to as YMAPP. YOU'RE MISSING A PIECE OF PAPER. That was the state of mind we adopted from our reality. If you wanted to do something, people around you would turn your attention to that one particular thing you couldn't or didn't know how to do. And that was it. You were done. Everything afterwards was always about deficit or lack, and somehow it would always grow bigger and stronger than anything you knew or had.

I remember I constantly laid traps to hold myself back. I would sabotage myself by thinking, "If only I had this or if only I knew that." What I was left with was the belief that life was a privilege that could only happen by chance.

My husband didn't see his co-worker for quite some time. Because of my longer school summer breaks, he took days off to be with me, and upon his arrival back at work, that young man was on leave.

I had already forgotten about that episode when he brought up the young man's name at the dinner table. Along with a good meal, I heard a great story about his colleague's experience of London. Not only that he drank beer in a British pub, but that he crossed paths with a girl who was travelling though England. She was also from Zagreb, and they returned home as a couple.

"Yes!" my face lit up with a smile. "Another one who escaped from the net!" I bet that young guy would never have dreamed that on the western side of his hometown, as if following a soccer match, an unknown woman acknowledged his brilliant act, cheering at the top of her lungs.

I also had friends in Zagreb who reminded me of something I frequently swept under the rug and thought was just me. Before the war, they were also young teenagers as I was, and they would suck up to their older friends in hopes they'd introduce them to the bigger world out there. But before they could even stand on their own, that life was gone. They couldn't find their place in the new world, nor could they mingle with the new crowd, so they learned to disconnect. They didn't even realize how far they'd gone.

I used to share with them my thoughts and feelings about the new places I discovered in Zagreb. For quite some time, my new home remained a mystery to me.

"Today, I went to a classical music concert." A good friend of mine was a student of the Academy of Music,[59] and I often went to listen to her performances. "It was heaven!" I told them, "I don't even know where to begin." I loved every piece of this event, which had left a great impression on me. "The concert hall was magical; it reminded me of the part of history I learned about while studying literature. I felt like I was preparing for an exam in romanticism." I babbled about the street in the historical centre of Zagreb. "I don't know how I missed it. Anyway, how come none of you told me to go there?" I stopped my monologue abruptly.

---

59 The oldest and the largest music school in Croatia, founded in 1829. The school became a part of the University of Zagreb in 1979.

My friends sat across from me, looking at each other and keeping quiet as though frozen in place.

"I don't know which concert hall you mean," one friend said to me at last, shrugging his shoulders. "Maybe we went there on a school trip," his wife, who was also from Zagreb said as she tried to remember.

They shook their heads, and we all fell silent. As I'd experienced many times before, I felt I was touching on something no one except me cared about. I was relieved when someone changed the topic.

After dinner, on our way back home, I told my husband in the car, "My sister's right. Me and my stupid stories, I can't seem to get rid of them." I was a little angry with myself. "As if I don't have anything to talk about with our friends, I have to bug them with things that don't interest them."

"Relax." He thought I was exaggerating.

A week passed, or maybe more, since we'd gotten together. Of course, I hadn't forgotten that conversation, but I hoped my friends had. I was more than surprised by what they shared the next time we met.

"I have to tell you something. Last time, after you told us that story about the concert hall, we stayed up late talking. In the morning, we cancelled our plans, picked up our daughter, and went downtown. I don't even know what we were expecting. We spent the whole day walking around. We showed her the park, the square, the monuments, the fountain, some streets. We had a great time. I hadn't even realized how much I have missed those moments. Or that I even needed them. It was such a good feeling." Goosebumps crept across my skin as he continued. "Thank you. I don't know how you did it, but you managed to connect me to my city again." I smiled. "It's strange, you're not from here. I don't know how to explain this to myself."

"I'm so glad to hear that!" I replied. "I feel you've just given me a compliment. You couldn't have thought up a better one."

If only he knew how hard it was for me to hear him say that. I was afflicted with the same condition: disconnection. I went silent as images of Belgrade flashed through my mind. I always remembered the good ones first and usually thought I was hard on my country and my fellow citizens. But then, I recalled all the harsh situations and circumstances, and they sobered me up in a second. All I could see in them were walls, high walls around me; all I could feel was pain. Something had broken inside, I knew, something I couldn't revive.

It was spring 2011, exactly forty-eight months after we applied, when my husband and I finally got our visas for Canada. I couldn't believe it.

My new departure plans weren't a surprise, even for those who didn't know about our application. With everything I'd experienced in Croatia, I felt like I was another person, yet in many ways the same. I wanted more independence, more options, and above all, a safer environment.

At the end of summer, our suitcases were packed, accounts closed, and checkouts made at the police station. We spent the last days with our families, who were still struggling to accept our decision.

Saying goodbye to Zagreb wasn't easy for me.

"Where do you find the strength?" one of my friends asked. "You're wrapping up your life here and packing as if it's nothing, and I know you're aware of how much that demands of a person." She sympathized with me.

"After all these years I know one thing for sure," I told her. "Whenever I would leave and see my old life dissolved, I would be able to regenerate. It was always hard, but I somehow found the strength to make my life up again."

It was much later that I understood this in another way. Every time I would leave the Balkans and familiar environments, my inner tension would lessen. I felt lighter and motivated to explore my options. I experienced a life that was broader and more diverse than the one I'd left behind.

I encountered various existential problems on my journey, many of which sucked up my time and energy. But they never discouraged me. I wasn't thinking about my struggles being pointless or myself not being capable of facing them. I stayed in the game, keeping away from toxicity and negative self-talk. I didn't stand in my own way.

CHAPTER TEN
Starting Anew

My father was born in a small village, 350 kilometres away from Belgrade; his family had lived there for generations. When I was growing up, my father told me many stories about his life journey and how he created a completely new life from scratch.

"I still remember the very moment when I stood at the top of Knez-Mihailova Street." Like many visitors, he went to see this beautiful and well-known pedestrian street in Belgrade's downtown. "I looked at those tall buildings, listened to the sounds of the city, and watched people go by. I had to hide my eyes from so many lights! Do you know what a scene like that meant to a kid like me?"

This was the story of my father's first trip to Belgrade. He came by train, with his brother and an acquaintance, to ask around about continuing his education in the country's capital. Much more significant than any of the information he collected was the impression he took home. He promised himself he'd return one day.

"I was in my own country," he told me, "but it seemed like I was in another world. I felt dizzy, as if the whole city was spinning." He gestured with his hands to illustrate how confused and excited he was. "I could see the road opening before me."

He couldn't have known where it would take him, but nothing could stop him from making small steps forward. Staying determined and courageous, as I did years later, he embraced an unknown world that helped him become the person he was destined to be.

For me, another world starts with every new chapter of life. Its frequent novelty is what makes it quite challenging and therefore tiring. At the beginning, one tends to feel restless as there are too many questions without answers. A great amount of energy has to be burned taking baby steps, one after another, day by day. No wonder people become easily frustrated and impatient, especially in situations when they are experiencing difficulties and pushbacks.

Whenever I moved to another country, I had to go through that process. After landing, the most important thing for me was to look for any kind of job which would bring me some sense of security. I would work at anything while I searched for better options. Many times, I found myself in circumstances neither I, nor anyone I knew, could have ever imagined.

Upon our arrival in Canada, my husband had a few job interviews over the phone. He'd nearly been hired by a surveillance company in Vancouver, when a friend got him a face-to-face interview at a Victoria-based company that analyzed power lines. At that time, we spent all our time together, as we were still completely reliant on each other. When he had his interview, I accompanied him to the office. While I was waiting in the lobby, I played with a dog that, it would later turn out, belonged to one of the company's managers. The pretty dog almost sat in my lap, without any intention of giving up on her cuddles, when the door to an office opened; my husband came out, followed by a young man.

He smiled at me and said in passing, "Hello, and you are?"

"I'm waiting for him," I gestured towards my husband, who'd already begun to say, "That's my wife."

"Nice to meet you," he nodded, and without pausing, continued, "And are you looking for a job too?"

I thought he was joking, so I just smiled. Maybe during the interview they'd been talking about how we'd arrived in Canada three weeks earlier and that our entire life was still up in the air.

"I'm not joking," he said.

I wasn't sure if I understood him correctly, yet I knew what he had just said. Even though I sometimes feel like the heroine from an overly exciting, as yet unread novel, this particular chapter still surprised me.

"Do you know how to work on a computer?" he asked. "We've got a huge backlog of work, and we're happy to give a job to anybody who's ready to start training straight away." He gestured to a space where people worked in little cubicles. "Come with me, and I'll show you what it is all about."

I exchanged a glance with my husband and stepped forward. I followed the manager to where a young man sat at a desk with two monitors. He was examining the wires on power lines and, by moving his mouse, he rotated the three-dimensional picture. I watched in awe. My knowledge of computers until then had included nothing more advanced than writing e-mails, surfing the net, and making assignments or course plans and programmes for school. This job looked like too great a challenge for my paltry knowledge of technology.

"There, you see it's nothing too scary." The manager sounded like a salesperson now, who wanted to convince even an uninterested customer to buy his product. "You'd learn it all after a week or so. You'd go through every step of the training process, just like everybody else did at this company, so it's not required to know these things ahead of time. If you want to try, here's your chance." I felt a little panicked, but I nodded yes, as I knew only a mad person would reject such a golden job opportunity.

"Don't worry. Computers are very simple toys," my husband said as soon as we stepped out onto the street. We'd been given confirmation that in a week or two we'd both be starting our new jobs together. I remained quiet, and my husband wanted to cheer me up. "Anyway, you'll soon ask yourself how you lived before you became dependent on computers. You're a creature of the twenty-first century, after all," he joked, alluding to what my father preached about being technically literate.

"You may not believe it, but I'm not even thinking about that," I replied as we walked back towards the house where we'd been staying. Adrenaline pumped through my body, and I became sober-minded. All that mattered was that I had a job and that our near future didn't seem uncertain anymore.

I grew up in a place where people did the same job their entire lives, most often in a single place. Somewhere along the way, I'd stopped worrying about whether my career deviations had gotten me lost and driven me to irresponsibly waste my time and energy. I changed my attitude, because I understood that every time I'd been rerouted, it had given me many new realizations and the chance to, as I like to say, round out some parts of my personality.

I mastered skills I had thought didn't come naturally to me, and this made my life a whole lot easier. I had the opportunity to express my practical side in a hundred different ways. I learned from my attempts and mistakes, and I progressed with every challenging situation. Most importantly, I worked with people I wouldn't have otherwise met. I stumbled into other professions and encountered co-workers who had different interests and life habits. This widened the limits of my world as I learned to look over them or beyond them.

Despite many disadvantages, job-related or not, there's an important advantage for anybody who enters a society without understanding its cultural norms. Newcomers approach everything more openly or, even better, without prejudice and rigidity. In this way, one can explore or uncover new possibilities.

When I moved to Zagreb, for instance, I didn't know that the Serbian Orthodox Church in Croatia had reopened a private school a few years earlier. No one I knew back then had a clue this school had existed in downtown Zagreb since the 19th century.

I simply ignored all the assumptions that there wasn't a need for a Serbian language teacher, and I searched on the Internet. I came across the name of this school with a job opening. I immediately dialled the number, but nobody answered. The next day, I went in person to the address listed.

"The job's been posted," the school principal said. "You should apply. We'll contact you with the results after the School Board meeting." I sent in all the necessary documentation and waited. Sure enough, they hired me.

I worked at that school for four years and learned how to be a good teacher. Over the years I spent in Croatia, that job allowed me to open many doors. I taught my mother tongue to a girl from a foreign country, who was preparing to live and work in Serbia. I also moonlighted for a local foreign language school, where I gave exams to future court interpreters. Another time, I translated hotel brochures for a company that was expanding their business in Serbia. All these jobs were stimulating and helped me to expand personally and professionally in ways I couldn't have imagined.

Life in a new place always starts with survival struggles, which is a necessary first step, and then it evolves into something else. I'd been through this experience so many times that I came to understand how, with that second step, lives that appear similar on the surface can separate and drift apart forever. This is partly of our own making and also a matter of some circumstances outside of our control.

I'd never lived in a culture that was so different from my own that my very appearance would make me stand out, rather than just my words or actions. Somehow, I was also led to settle in larger cities or popular tourist locations, which are, by their nature, transient. As if I was in my natural habitat, among so many others from various places and different walks of life, I would look around for clues and make my own way.

Different societies gradually broadened my horizons and reshaped me from the inside. I discovered I wasn't alone in this process, as I met individuals of other races, nations, and cultures who were experiencing the same thing. Once I heard an official from Japan explaining this in a way that really resonated with me. Asked to list all the places and attractions people should visit in order to get to know their own country, he unexpectedly replied, "If you really want to know your surroundings, get out."

Once I had encountered a range of different mentalities, it was easier for me to shed light on the patterns of living and thinking I'd adopted in my own society. By immersing myself in new things, I grasped the unknown and, more importantly, I started to question the so-called familiar. It was throughout this process that I truly began to understand what my father referred to as another world. My head was spinning from this newly discovered space.

When I was first introduced to Croatian society, it was in many ways similar to the one I came from. I was familiar with the social issues and habits, and able to make tighter bonds with people with whom I already shared similar childhoods, upbringings, personal interests, and values. Within a year, I'd created my own universe, which was all I needed to accept a new place as home.

On the other hand, all this sameness made it easier to spot the differences which shook me up and motivated me to change some of my behaviours. I accepted a new way of communicating and approaching problems, a different professional code, and an increased responsibility with money matters. All of that led me towards greater self-awareness and independence of mind. After some time, I had the impression I'd been walking around with my head in the clouds, but now I could finally see where I was and where I could go next.

As a newcomer, both in Croatia and Cyprus, I was exposed to a wider and more diverse group of people than ever before, both from my new society and from my country of origin. At first, I had to deal with a lot of discomfort and conflicted emotions, but after a while, this became the most rewarding position of all. Acknowledging where others had come from, and understanding how they were shaped within their different nations, generations, classes, and professions, helped me put in place the missing pieces of reality and life I had always struggled to comprehend.

From this new perspective, I became more thankful for the things I'd overlooked or taken for granted, like my carefree childhood, affordable schooling, and well-meaning companions. As I got to know people from other countries who were around my age, it became clearer to me how the war and years of isolation had affected my emotional development and experience of life. Accustomed to constantly evaluating social values or questioning the goals people put on a pedestal, I may have come across as a wiser person and more insightful than many. But then, like a child, I also felt envious of their privilege to go through the process of maturing recklessly, without rushing. I grieved that loss for years.

In Croatia and Cyprus, I needed time to make friends. Once I did, I enjoyed sharing time and energy with them. The locals instantly relaxed in my presence, feeling free of the judgement that had been forced on them by their society and fellow citizens. Ever-present unrealistic expectations didn't allow them to see how much they had already accomplished and achieved. They found a sympathetic listener in me, someone who could understand them and accept them for who they were.

The newcomers, meanwhile, had the same concerns I did, so despite our differences, we could effortlessly relate to each other. I think a fresh start in a new country gave all of us the opportunity to approach one another without hesitation and to show compassion and humility when needed.

When I first encountered North American society, I had quite a different experience, as I found novelties even in places I wasn't expecting them. For example, to rent an apartment, I needed a verbal or written recommendation, as well as proof of employment. When I finally did move in, I wouldn't find it furnished, and very quickly I would also learn my electricity bill had to be registered under my name.

It took me a while to accept that my professional life would be an ongoing process of relearning and adapting. My diploma, which I'd needed to emigrate, didn't actually mean much. I had to either upgrade or find a new career course. I had found a job, which I experienced as a stroke of luck, but it turned out to be just one tiny piece of a much larger puzzle. I needed to get used to working evening shifts that ended at 1 am, in addition to constantly learning about things of which I had no prior knowledge.

"What the heck is a root folder?" I asked my husband in the early morning hours after coming home. I couldn't wrap my head around Micro Station and any of the computer tools I had to use for my daily tasks.

These professional challenges were amplified by cultural differences. I worked next to people from all over the world: Russia, New Zealand, Israel, Germany, India, Britain, as well as locals of various ethnic and cultural backgrounds. Although interacting regularly, we remained somewhat distanced for months and even years. Building bridges takes time, and it has to come from the willingness of both parties.

When I wasn't at work, I rushed from one store to another, buying furniture that we needed for our household. Every day, I learned about the sales at the local markets and food shops. I also had to find time to prepare for my driver's test. Days passed as I got to know the new rules. I wondered why I was allowed to turn right at a red light. Then my husband informed me he'd bought a second-hand car. "There's just one tiny thing which is different," he said calmly. I protested, not wanting to hear it. "You need to know. We're going to be driving an automatic."

My old life was unravelling at such a pace I wasn't always able to hold myself together. Driving was something I'd always enjoyed doing, yet I had never driven an automatic car.

"I can't stand this anymore," I repeated often, feeling as if I was being attacked by the rest of the world. In those moments, taking a shower or going for long walks seemed to be the only escape I had which would grant me some sort of relaxation.

Over the next few months, I went deeper into the differences between my new and old reality. There was a lot I didn't understand, so both consciously and unconsciously I judged it.

How is it possible that you can hardly wait to escape the city centre? In Europe, everything — shopping, entertainment, and restaurants — is focused in the downtown area. Living in suburbs or putting effort into outdoor activities wasn't something I appreciated at the beginning.

That's not coffee! You're not supposed to drink it with liquor, a bunch of spices or special creams, especially not while strolling down the street. My favourite time alone always went with a plain cup of coffee in my hands, when I would read newspapers or books, or just daydream. In Canada, I continued doing that, but I missed having intimate conversations with friends over the hot coffee. Every little detail, from welcoming people at my place, to cooking coffee on a stove, serving it on a tray, and watching a person's eyes, was suddenly gone.

I worked with a colleague who sat two desks away from me in the same room, yet our work-related conversations were always electronic. It's hard to believe today, but I struggled to not take this impersonal approach personally.

Men or women, Canadians love to hug. I discovered that's the way they express many emotions like happiness, sorrow, worry, surprise, and appreciation. Many times, I would end up in someone's arms, which I thought was weird. Before coming to Victoria, I was more into shaking hands, nodding my head, touching a shoulder, or smiling. I didn't want to get physically close to somebody I didn't know well.

Time management was another issue. I knew

it was all about using time wisely and trying out new things, but the way people here organized their vacation seemed more like training for the Olympics than going on a deserved holiday. Isn't the point of a holiday to set yourself free of any routine and just enjoy being in the moment?

It was such a relief to meet other immigrants who were going through a process similar to mine. I could say that I'd never felt so close to other Europeans as I did in that first year in Canada. Many times, we had the same observations regarding social interactions or self-presentation, and we found ourselves walking around questioning which foot goes where.

I found that no culture, class, or profession was an exception to the matters of this process. Everybody needs time to stop, rethink, evaluate, and adjust to new circumstances. Some people, even after years and years of living in a different country, struggle to perceive new situations without harsh judgement. We're conditioned by the boundaries of the society and the culture we come from more than we are ready to admit, and the ones who hang on rigidly to their old behaviours always clash with the others.

I don't remember the moment when I turned my attention from those exterior differences to human-to-human interactions. Little by little, I understood I was on the same page as so many others. For example, I worked the same shift as people who were all, more or less, facing the same beginner's challenges in the professional world as I was. For most of them, this was also an unfamiliar job, and on top of that, for some Canadians, Victoria was also an adopted home, and in many ways a new environment.

Other times, I found myself in situations where I'd run into people who were once in my shoes. I remember one gentleman when we were waiting in the theatre for the film to start. He approached my husband and me after he heard us talking in our language. He was right when he assumed we spoke one of the Slavic languages, as his parents did. As we were still new to the city and often quite alone, we mentioned our struggle to find our own tribe. He advised us to join a society in Victoria.

"Sooner or later relationships crystallize," I rushed to reply. "I don't like to force things."

"Forget the European view of socializing. Here you can do anything with anybody. You just have to change your approach. Follow your interests," he said confidently. But that was maybe an issue, too. Once you are in a process of change, besides the things you don't like, you start examining the things you do like. It's more complicated than it appears to be. "But if you want to stick to the old continent," he was eager to help us find a solution, "there are various European societies. I'd recommend the Scots or the Ukrainians. They're the most cheerful."

"But I'm not Scottish or Ukrainian." The idea of being in that situation amused me.

"My parents went through the same uncertainties as you. You'd be surprised how things work here. And how many similarities you might uncover along the way. Give it a try!"

In the end, my story about finding my crew happened entirely spontaneously. I managed to put it together while attending my Canadian citizenship ceremony in 2015.

To become a Canadian, I needed to do all sorts of things. I had to secure permanent residency, wait for several years, sit a language test, and prove my presence in this new country. Eventually, I had to pass an exam on history, geography, the Constitution, and Canadian identity, and then wait to be called to take an Oath of Citizenship.

Citizenship ceremonies happen once or twice a year in Victoria, and for me, who had never had an opportunity to even see one before, it was an event I waited for with excitement. The closing part was strictly ceremonial and went as expected with music, welcome speeches by a few government officials, photos, and cake. But the other part, the one which preceded the ceremony itself, was a real treat to me.

All the future citizens were participants in roundtable discussions led by a representative of the organizer. There were eight tables that day, and we were seated at one of them. There were people from Australia, Vietnam, China, Mexico, and the USA. The second of the three questions opened up a discussion on the theme of belonging to a new country, and it had a clear aim. The question was, "Tell us if you've ever felt that you belonged here, and if so, when was it?"

While I waited for my turn to speak, I listened to the others carefully. I learned that some had found new hobbies and forged strong connections with the members of those groups, while others had started their own businesses and discovered their first shared language with their colleagues and clients. Yet many relied on the support of an individual and societies from their home countries, who had helped them navigate through the unknown territory.

And then everybody looked at me.

"I began to build a strong connection to my new country when I had a baby." Even though I didn't speak of anything unusual, some people were surprised.

It was when I was pregnant that I stopped feeling like someone who'd come from somewhere else. I suddenly had a lot in common with many others. The first place I felt a sense of closeness was in a prenatal centre, where I connected with a group of expectant mothers. Then, at work, I started talking more and more with people who were parents or who had newborns in their families. Barriers kept falling away on their own as my belly got rounder. At the doctor's and the dentist's offices, I met people who acted as though we were close and newfound members of the same family.

Later, with a baby in my arms, my relationship with strangers on the street changed, too. They came up to me, asked all sorts of questions, made comments, and shared so much useful information. Thanks to them, I discovered new and interesting places, activities, and other parents. I took my chance and approached them with more trust.

In a few months, I'd become a part of a community of parents from all over the world: the Philippines, China, Japan, Mexico, India, Spain, France, Portugal, and Canada. We made playdates together, went to story times at local libraries, attended workshops and summer festivals, and enjoyed beach time. In this game of motherhood, we all had something to learn from one another. I kept my eyes and ears open as I absorbed things that seemed stimulating. Meanwhile, I was surprised at how willing people were to try and take on the things I'd brought with me.

The gentleman from the movie theatre had indeed been right. By getting deeper into my new community, I was delighted to discover how much we had in common. I recognized the same familial conditions and gender roles in the cultures of the Far East, the same way of living in numerous European, Central American, and South American nations, and the same attitude towards education and self-expression in the older generations from North America. Despite our different pasts and backgrounds, we all had to navigate through unknown territory and looked for ways to deal with the demands of an unforeseeable reality. Bit by bit, I no longer withheld myself or hesitated to speak my truth. It was quite the opposite. I would step out into the world with a strong sense of belonging and inner knowing that I was, in fact, a meaningful and inseparable part of this huge human tribe.

CHAPTER ELEVEN
Beginning to Heal

I was never one of those girls who dreamed about being a mother one day. As a young woman, I was so disappointed by humanity that I used to say I had no intention of keeping the mess around. And for many years, I hadn't even thought or talked about it.

It was easier for me to push back on societal pressure and expectation than to resist an enormous inner desire to have a child. It came in Canada, along with the wave of other changes that altered my life to its core. Out of nowhere, this longing slipped in under the layers and layers of thoughts and experiences, and I started envisioning my new life.

Thank God I wasn't going through this important transition on my own. My husband was beside me. There wasn't a single part of my pregnancy, which I called *our* pregnancy, when he wasn't by my side supporting me. Together we found a doctor, went to appointments and check-ups, read through test results, and lived through uncertainties, renovations, and the birth. From the beginning, we were aware of the changes that would enter our lives when the baby came, and later on, we shared the responsibilities of our new reality. This helped both him and me to build a strong connection with our child, and it also strengthened our own relationship through mutual understanding and support.

During the weekdays, like most mothers, I spent a lot of time alone with my child, completely focused on her demands and needs. It was as if my days fell into a pattern of sleeping, feeding, walking, and bathing, and then the whole process would start all over again. I accepted this new situation without resistance and tuned out the noise of the world around me. Occasionally, I would go to the park. We celebrated one or two Canadian summer holidays, but mostly I spent time between doctor's appointments taking long walks through my neighbourhood.

As time went on, everything became livelier. We moved to a new building, which was full of young kids, and had exactly the atmosphere we needed at that moment. My daughter soon took her first independent steps, and we entered a new, much busier phase by doing a variety of indoor and outdoor activities. My daily life was bursting with interactions with other parents and toddlers, and for months, I didn't have time to wonder how it was affecting me.

It was when my child was a year and a half old that I became aware of the changes in my way of life and thinking. I'd fallen into them so naturally that I couldn't explain them even to myself.

For example, we'd be sitting in the park or on the beach, and from the outside, it looked like we weren't doing anything. My daughter would start playing with the grass or the sand and remained focused and entertained for long periods of time. Completely entranced, she'd turn things over and over, from one side to the other. She'd pick things up with her two little hands and throw them, with a wonder and excitement that I couldn't help but notice.

"What's that, my darling?" I'd ask her, and she'd answer by babbling and smiling. I'd spend the entire time revelling in this sight.

I described this moment to my husband later, as if it was some great scene from a famous movie, one of those that stick in your head forever. Carried away by the impression, I missed that it went deeper than I thought.

I slowed myself down. I stopped rushing around like a blue-arsed fly and beating myself up with a never-ending list of things to do. Something switched inside, as I could decide more easily what things I would or wouldn't do. I felt more relaxed and immersed in every moment that was before me. I relished the changing of the seasons, the tree-lined streets I walked down, the friendly conversations with our landlord, and the gestures or smiles of passers-by. Even those small family moments I didn't use to appreciate, I now found to be significant and powerful, like going for groceries, making lunch, bath times, singing, playing with blocks, or waving to the Moon. The world became new as I discovered our own unique language and the opportunity to get closer at the end of each day. I couldn't have predicted how much strength and happiness I would draw from it.

In my daughter's presence, I lost my harsh streak of seriousness and suddenly became childlike, something I hadn't been for years. I crawled across the floor, slid under the table, hid behind my hands, or pulled faces. We were together everywhere: on the swings, in the sand, climbing onto the slide, and dancing to music. I entertained her with tickles, or tricked her by taking one of her toys from her hands. I stole her snacks, and hid woodchips in my pockets or on my head. I did everything I could just to see her smile and, like a kiss, that smile would light up my face as well.

Because of my daughter, my inner energy was now focused on understanding and support, and that transferred into my relationships with others. Rigid barriers crumbled as my attitude and my manner became softer and quieter. I no longer hurried to make assumptions or unassailable conclusions. I let every encounter develop according to the situation. With no clear intentions to do so, I was considerate and friendly to everyone. And in return, people reacted the same way to me, which brought me the sense of peace and union I had sought for a long time.

I felt so refreshed by this new way of being that I had an impulse to recreate my life. For months, I patiently questioned many of the choices I'd made until then, like the details of my daily routine of feeding and exercising, my needs, responsibilities, and activities. I researched new options and acted upon them as I finally had the ability to make changes. I had more resources than ever before, as well as professionals I could go to for help. I told myself that now was the perfect time. I didn't think about obstacles or restrictions. Led by the thought that I was establishing new foundations and an encouraging atmosphere for my child's progress and mine, I had no plan to give up, despite the constant fatigue that came with being a mother. I gave myself time, and as the results became more and more evident, I felt as if I'd just disembarked onto a new continent.

What could I focus my energy on, I asked myself, without worrying about what was already behind me? Career-wise, I went back to the drawing board to rethink my possibilities and wishes. I joined an international language school, booked an appointment with a career counsellor, and sent out my resume for various jobs. I also put my name down to volunteer at the Victoria Film Festival.

"Bring back play!" I heard a Canadian TV ad one day, and I couldn't get it out of my head. It was as if it had been plucked from our world and dropped onto the small screen.

Emphasizing the importance of physical activity for kids' development, the ad showed a range of images of boys and girls who were splashing each other with water, running around, playing hide-and-seek, and riding bikes. "Get moving," was its message. "There's health, happiness, and strength waiting for you."

That advertisement made me think about all the phases my daughter was going through. Well, yes, every one of them was exactly that. **Play**, I thought. She started playing, first off, with her fingers and toes. Then it was her food. She played with my jewellery, with bags, or with toys. Finally, I watched with joy as she began using her body to interact with the world.

Our everyday lives suddenly became so bright and colourful that we stopped caring what time of year it was, whether we had any plans or not, if we had anyone to play with, or even if we could. So what if it was raining, or if it was six in the evening and we were alone in the park? Who cares if we didn't bring chalk or a bucket and a spade?

My daughter was one of those kids who took giant strides into new spaces and shaped them with her presence. She'd run into the sand or to the playground and spontaneously join the group. I rarely had to interfere, and if I did, it was mostly because of the language barrier. Soon after, I enrolled her in a local dance studio, where we danced alongside other moms and toddlers. When she wanted a bike, we could be found learning to ride on the road.

My favourite event was when she won over the local water taxi drivers. She waved to them from the shore and blew kisses, to which they responded by blasting their horns. On the boat, she'd sit on the front deck without any fear, which helped her get a bunch of smiles, a handful of badges, and a sticker proclaiming her a real islander.

"That's me," I said to my husband one day, while we were watching her running through the park with kids.

"You mean she reminds you of you when you were a kid?" he asked.

"Absolutely." I felt as though I was losing my sense of time and space. My daughter's childhood reminded me of mine and also of the faces and places I hadn't been able to connect with for such a long time. And now, just like that, they started coming into the light again. "But I'm thinking of something else too. Look at all those children! It's as if some amazing energy is carrying them around." I didn't know how to describe it, but I could sense that pulse somewhere inside me.

I was giving my daughter more and more freedom, and she liked it.

"Now, Mommy, I'm going to teach you how to talk on the phone." She took every opportunity to show me how much she'd grown. "You pick it up like this, and you press the button." She banged on the dial pad, saying words without meaning.

"Right. And what language are you speaking?" I asked her, interested.

"English," she replied seriously.

"Good." I nodded. "Can I make a call now? We need to call your big sister."

That big sister is her favourite friend. My daughter has several and loves them all, but this one is special. There's a ten-year age gap, but whether it's because her parents speak Serbian or some other reason, she tells everyone that this girl is her sister.

"I'll ring her," she insisted. "You still have to grow up," she explained.

"Well, when am I finally going to grow up?" I acted concerned.

"After five minutes and two broccolis." She was very serious.

"Agreed." I let her finish her game.

Her imagination was caught by any story in which the heroine shared her name. We started by rewriting the famous ones. One day, she was the third little pig, the clever one that had made a house out of bricks and beaten the wolf, and the next day she'd be brave little Thumbling[60] who faced the giant and stole his seven-league[61] boots. We also made up a new story with her name, and she boasted that she'd saved Christmas by turning on all the lights around the house to illuminate the foggy, festive night.

Her room was our stage. One day it would be an airport, the next a beach. We set up a tent in the middle of it, and I wasn't allowed to move a single thing.

"That's not paper," she let me know. "They are Ginger's diapers." Ginger was her first teddy bear. "He's going on a trip tomorrow, so I got some ready for him." She shoved Ginger into a basket.

I loved to watch her sink into a world where nothing was impossible. She used her imagination freely and expressed herself in a way I found very alluring. I rushed to join her in that limitless space as I started telling my stories. Many of them gave me a chance to convince her to do something she didn't want to do. Back then, she would refuse to eat the meat in her soup, so I made her believe that every bird that sat on the roofs of the neighbouring houses was just sitting and waiting for the right moment to steal her food.

---

60 A story of seven sons abandoned in the woods by their parents. The youngest son found a way back home by stealing boots from a giant. He helped the king's soldiers capture the giant, and the King gave the boy a bag of golden coins as a prize. The brothers returned home safely.

61 A common item in European folklore; the boots allow a person wearing them to take strides of seven leagues per step, resulting in great speed. A league equals 2.2 km or 1.4 miles.

"The minute you turn around, there'll be a cracking sound." I acted as if they were all playing in a live show. "You do what you want, but be aware she'll fly the meat across the ocean to Granny. She won't leave anything for you." She'd snap out of it and eat everything on her plate.

And as for seagulls? We had one that was kind of ours. It always waited for us at the park. For a long time, my daughter had learned to share food and toys with her friends, so I wanted her to demonstrate she could do the same for our seagull. I asked her to leave a piece of bread or two for him on the curb, so he'd have a snack. "You remember, we have to think about other creatures, right? Maybe he didn't have time to buy his snack, but he managed to come to the park to meet us." She would nod and take a few pretzels out of her container.

Another time we listened to his cries, and since she was used to me translating the conversations I would have with people in English, she asked what the seagull was saying. I laughed at first, and then an idea popped into my head.

"He's asking where you've been." And then I stopped to hear what else he had to say. "Well, he's begging you to hurry up with your breakfast next time. Your playtime is running out!" And she promised she would.

I ventured into every day as if it was my last. Even though our days were completely ordinary, each one invigorated me beyond measure. I spent the mornings and early afternoons with my daughter wherever our paths would take us and with people we met along the way. In the afternoons, I'd work in front of the computer, checking the wiring of the world's power lines with greater interest. And in the middle of one such afternoon, a question occurred to me.

"What wouldn't I do to keep this day forever?"

It was so precious to me. It kept me from thinking that in a world full of despair, this much joy wasn't real. Somehow, I was no longer afraid of the idea we're going down a path where everything in front of us was as promising as it was terrifying. I made peace with the fact that today I was alive and able to create all those wonderful memories of ours but, by the time some other tomorrow rolled around, I might not be next to her anymore.

And the answer to my question came when I was volunteering at the Victoria Film Festival. I was working as a host's assistant at a downtown exhibition room, where people could come, check out the antique cameras, and watch silent movies.

One afternoon, a foreigner stepped in. He was an inventor himself and initially wanted to check out the vintage gear. After browsing for a little while, he came to my desk to pick up flyers, and we started chatting. We spoke about films, old times, and the world's changes; then he asked me about my vocation. I mentioned how I was struggling to find my professional path, especially now that I was a recent immigrant. I told him I had always longed to find something I could do regardless of external circumstances. I suddenly blurted out, "I truly enjoy sharing life experiences with people from different worlds." Then I added, "I would talk with them and do my best to bring those separate worlds together so others can cherish them like I do. Mm-hmm?" And I stopped, as a thought came to my mind. "Maybe I could also write about it?"

I had never thought of writing, not even when I was a literature student. I was somehow convinced writing wasn't my thing.

"So, why don't you do that then?" he asked, and I added a dozen *buts*.

I went home and thought about it again. My curiosity became bigger than my doubts.

"Bring back play!" I said, as I lowered my hands to the keyboard and started to write this book.

I didn't have a clue where writing would take me, only the belief it was what I needed to do. In a split second, the memory of a long-gone weekend came back to me. I saw myself as a girl of seven or eight sitting at the dining room table and finishing her Sunday breakfast. She gazed at the clock on the wall, carefully checking the time. The night before, at the playground, all the kids from the neighbourhood had agreed to meet in front of the building, no later than nine in the morning. This little girl didn't want to be late. She had to arrive to that morning's roll call on time. Otherwise, she wouldn't get onto a team. No way! She didn't want to sit and wait for another game to start.

Acknowledgments

I dedicate this book to my daughter, Irina Helena Sekulic. Although I learned that writing this book was something I had to do for myself, her presence was a strong motivator to start this journey and also the biggest force propelling me forward. *"I find comfort in knowing we will always be able to meet each other along these lines."*

I am grateful to my husband, Nikica Sekulic, for supporting our family life and ensuring I have the time and energy for (re)writing. *"Without you, I wouldn't have been able to complete this journey."*

I want to send special thanks to the people who took part in creating this book. As a self-publisher I depended on their hard work and support:

To Sarah Rengel, the first translator of my book in the Serbian language. *"This time we weren't able to make it until the end, but, who knows, we might cross paths again in the future."*

To Darcy Nybo, my trustworthy editor. *"Your every comment was listened to and valued. Without your guidance I wouldn't have been able to complete* this task and find satisfaction in the final product. I appreciate everything I've learned during our collaboration."

To Iryna Spica, the designer of my book. *"It is good to know I can always count on you. Thank you for being there for me."*

To my early readers: Scott Hamerton, an artist and my loyal coworker; Nikica Sekulic, my partner and biggest supporter; Shannon Perkins Carr, a music therapist and emerging author; Anthony Carr, an artist and a friend. *"Thank you for this collaboration. I appreciate your valuable feedback and encouragement. You rock!"*

To Norma J. Hill, Natasha Pashchenko, Shannon Perkins Carr, the proofreaders.

To the Perry-Castañeda Library Map Collection at the University of Texas at Austin.

About the Author

After Nataša Ćećez-Sekulić published her first book in the Serbian language (*Danas nam je divan dan*, 2018), she continued writing stories for her blog.

In spring 2020 she created an online cultural project, Liminal World, where she brings out the voices of people from different cultures, backgrounds, and mindsets in a set of video interviews. Participants share their life journeys and reflect on changes they have experienced during Covid-19.

The Journey to Bring Back Play (2021) is the English version of the book she originally wrote and published in Serbian.

Nataša Ćećez-Sekulić lives in Victoria, BC, Canada with her family.

www.natasacecezsekulicen.com
YouTube: Liminal World

www.ingramcontent.com/pod-product-compliance
Lightning Source LLC
Chambersburg PA
CBHW070348120526
44590CB00014B/1061